GREAT SPEECH!

A SIMPLE & PROVEN BLUEPRINT TO CRAFTING KEYNOTES & SIGNATURE TALKS

GREAT SPEECH!

A SIMPLE & PROVEN BLUEPRINT TO CRAFTING KEYNOTES & SIGNATURE TALKS

CESAR CERVANTES
&
STEVEN HAYWARD

ethos
collective

GREAT SPEECH! © 2025 by Cesar Cervantes & Steven Hayward.
All rights reserved.

Printed in the United States of America

Published by Igniting Souls
PO Box 43, Powell, OH 43065
IgnitingSouls.com

This book contains material protected under international and federal copyright laws and treaties. Any unauthorized reprint or use of this material is prohibited. No part of this book may be reproduced or transmitted in any form or by any means, electronic or mechanical, including photocopying, recording, or by any information storage and retrieval system, without express written permission from the author.

LCCN: 2024923441
Paperback ISBN: 978-1-63680-418-7
Hardcover ISBN: 978-1-63680-419-4
e-book ISBN: 978-1-63680-420-0

Available in paperback, hardcover, e-book, and audiobook.

Any Internet addresses (websites, blogs, etc.) and telephone numbers printed in this book are offered as a resource. They are not intended in any way to be or imply an endorsement by Igniting Souls, nor does Igniting Souls vouch for the content of these sites and numbers for the life of this book.

Some names and identifying details may have been changed to protect the privacy of individuals.

DEDICATION

To Katherine, Frances, Eddie, Jimmy, Campbell, and my mum, Phyllis, who first taught me to love public speaking and how to make a speech sing.
—Steve

To my loving wife Stephanie and my precious daughters, Isela and Fiona, without whom this book would have been completed two years earlier.
—Cesar

> There are two types of speakers:
> Those who get nervous and those who are liars.
>
> —Mark Twain

Table of Contents

Foreword 9
A Preface You Should Actually Read 13
   Who Are You Guys Anyway? 19
Chapter One: The Blueprint 23
Chapter Two: Attention-Getter 31
Chapter Three: Problem Statement 42
Chapter Four: Throughline 50
Chapter Five: Build the Problem 55
Chapter Six: Solutions 72
Chapter Seven: OMG Moment 83
Chapter Eight: Call to Action 92
Chapter Nine: The Secret Ingredient 96
Appendix: The Blueprint in Action 105
   Great Speech #1 106
   Great Speech #2 108
   Great Speech #3 111
   Great Speech #4 114
   Great Speech #5 117
Acknowledgments 119
About the Authors 121

Table of Contents

Foreword

By Comedian Leanne Morgan
Netflix Special: *I'm Every Woman*

When this little book first landed on my doorstep, I thought the folks who wrote it—God love 'em—had sent it to the wrong person. A book about public speaking? Me? I've always been able to talk, and even talk in public, but I'm long-winded and unorganized. Those two things don't always make for a great public speaker.

Here's the thing: just because you can talk in public, doesn't mean you know how to do it well. People think that, but it just isn't true. We've all been there, stuck in the audience, staring at the exit sign, dreaming about what we're going to eat for lunch. In the meantime, some poor soul is standing at a podium, droning on and on and on. Bless their hearts—it's not their fault. More likely than not, they didn't want to get up there in the first place. They can even feel themselves dragging it on and on. The idea that there's a way to do it, a blueprint for giving a speech that people will not just sit through but remember, is a new one.

As I started reading, it was like someone had turned on a light in a room I didn't even know was dark.

I realized that this book was something I should've had a long time ago. And by long ago, I mean way back when I first met Cesar in 2002—or was it 1492? Time flies when you're having fun and you've got brain fog. This was the early stand-up comedy days for me and Cesar—back when he had that beautiful curly hair and was cracking jokes about his Mexican mama. As for me, when I wasn't onstage or taking my kids to school, I was going into ladies' living rooms and selling jewelry. At least, that was what I was supposed to be doing. But somehow, instead of jewelry, I'd end up talking about anything and everything else, from breastfeeding to hemorrhoids and everything in between. Those ladies loved it, and they laughed, a lot, and once you get someone laughing, you can sell them most anything.

If I'd had this book back then, things might've been different. Maybe I would've known how to make them laugh and sell them jewelry. Maybe I would've understood the importance of transforming your audience. Which is really what this book is about.

Transforming your audience is what these gents mean by blueprint, or formula, or whatever label you want to print out and stick on the side of it. That's the gold in these pages. A blueprint sounds like a secret, but it's not. Not this kind of blueprint. It's something we all carry around with us, we just don't know it. It's that blueprint that tells you a great speech is great when you hear it. It's the same kind of thing like when I walked into a house our real estate agent showed us that had a hot tub in the middle of the living room. No one gave me the blueprint for a house I'd want to live in, but you know it when you see it.

You know what I love most about this book? It's not just about how to craft an argument, or how to talk about a problem so that people will care. It's a formula for connection. It's about finding common ground, that shared experience that makes people nod their heads and say, "SAME!" That's the real magic of humor and of public speaking, and this book brings them together. That's the blueprint this book hands over in a simple, straightforward way.

Whether you've been speaking for a while and you're looking to up your game, or you're just starting out and feeling so nervous you could faint, whether you're the keynote speaker or about to give your first TEDx talk, this book is for you. It's got the wisdom of experience, the practicality of a good sensible shoe, and enough humor to keep you from throwing it across the room.

And remember, whether you're selling jewelry in a home or doing stand-up in San Antonio, whatever you're doing—speaking, selling, or just trying to get your kids to eat their greens—make 'em laugh!

A Preface You Should Actually Read

After delivering, reviewing, writing, and editing literally thousands of speeches over the last twenty-plus years that have over 24 million views and hundreds of standing ovations, we've identified **three** primary problems our clients have:

1. **Structure**
   They don't know how to shape their talk for maximum impact.
2. **Writing**
   They envision their speech being as perfect and eloquent as the idea was in their minds, but writing isn't their strong suit, and they struggle to bring it to life on the page.
3. **Delivery**
   They're still developing the essential skills needed to step onstage and deliver their speech with power.

This book will focus on problem number one.

While all three elements are crucial, we're zeroing in on *structure* because (1) that's the foundation on which everything else is built, and (2) it's the *fastest* route to dramatic improvement of any speech. No matter what stage your speech is at or how much of a mess it seems, understanding how to *shape* it is going to result in a dramatic, immediate improvement.

Writing and delivery are crucial, no question, but they take *time* to develop and perfect, and there's usually a lot of fine-tuning, or tinkering—tweaking and re-tweaking small details—involved. On the other hand, understanding and implementing an effective structure can transform a speech *immediately*.

It's like the blueprint for a house—you might still need to get the right materials, or still learn to use a hammer, you might still need to *find* a hammer, but without a clear vision of how the whole house is going to look in the end, without a blueprint, it's going to be tough to construct a building anyone would want to live in.

Most of all, we wanted to write the kind of book we wanted to read—and which we *didn't* see out there already. There are already a number—and by "number," we mean literally hundreds—of books out there about writing and delivery. For as long as people have been writing, there have been other people telling them how to write and writing books of their own.

The same goes for delivery. There's a lot of excellent works dedicated to stage presence and vocal technique. It's all crucial and helpful, but we wanted to give readers something *essential*—a book clear enough that people could actually use it. When it comes to writing a great speech, beautiful language and great stage presence are nice to have, but neither is going to save a speech that's fundamentally misorganized.

A Preface You Should Actually Read

What's missing is a clear, practical guide to the underlying architecture of great speeches—the blueprint that makes them work. This is the gap the book you're holding fills.

There are many different kinds of speeches, but in this book we'll focus on two types that people tend to see as particularly high stakes, the kind that people *know* will take themselves and their message—their brand—to the next level: keynote speeches and TEDx talks.

The keynote speech and the TEDx talk have a lot in common, but they also differ from each other in some crucial ways, which we'll be getting into in more detail later. But in the interest of avoiding any confusion, we're going to start by outlining the basics of each form and also share how the term "signature talk" connects the two.

Keynote Speech: The term keynote really just means that you are, essentially, a big deal. You're the focus at the conference or event, the big show, the headliner, the grandmaster, the "hold the phone I can't believe you were able to book them at our event!" speaker.

The standard—and shorter—version of a keynote speech is about twenty to thirty minutes long, though it's common to get hired to fill in an hour slot or more. The classic (and most annoying) example of this is when you speak at the closing dinner of the event, or perhaps the dinner *is* the event, like a fundraiser.

We've never met a speaker who loves to hear they are speaking while people are eating, but the reality is that this happens all the time—even to highly paid big-name speakers or celebrities. It's also the case that when it comes to keynotes, there's a lot of variation depending on the nature of the event and the size of the group.

Sometimes, the keynote involves the speaker engaging the audience with interactive exercises that are related to the topic. Keynotes can also include visual aids—such as a slide deck or PowerPoint presentation. Ideally your keynote should be a speech that you can shrink or expand when you need to. We've helped clients give five-minute versions of their keynotes for particularly high-stakes meetings or even an ESPN interview.

The idea with the keynote is to craft a speech with flexibility baked into it. This is the talk you're going to give a version of whether you have ten minutes, twenty, or an hour to fill, in a context where you may or may not be required to engage with the audience at some level, and that will work as well with a group of twenty as it will with two thousand.

Signature Talk: Another term you'll often hear is "signature talk" or "signature speech." "Signature" just means that it's the talk you give whenever you're asked to deliver your core message—your "signature" idea that defines your work and impact. While not every signature talk originates from a TEDx talk, and not every keynote becomes your signature, the goal is to create a message so clear and powerful that it becomes synonymous with your brand and ultimately why you'll be paid to speak.

TEDx Talk: The TEDx form is more clearly defined, with a clear set of rules and guidelines that make it a particular challenge. First off, it's shorter. TED limits the length of all talks to no longer than eighteen minutes, but most are *much* shorter—our recommendation is that your TEDx talk come in at about ten to twelve minutes max.

We believe this shorter form can be powerful and transformational, and though *you* might feel like you could go on forever, or that the short form doesn't do your message justice, it can be helpful to imagine an audience that doesn't feel the same. Mastering this form sets the foundation for expanding into a keynote, workshops, retreats, books, and more.

It's also important for people to get to the *end* of your TEDx talk. It's much more likely for your talk to get traction on YouTube and result in more impact and views when your audience watches the whole thing.

No question, the length of the TEDx talk has varied over time—in the early days of TED, there were a number of *very* long talks that got a ton of views, but the platform, particularly the TEDx dimension of it, has evolved in a direction where clarity and conciseness are priorities. This shift reflects a deeper understanding of how ideas spread in our connected world. The TEDx format, with its emphasis on a single, transformative idea delivered with precision, has become the perfect laboratory for studying speech structure.

That's why we focus so much on TEDx in what follows. It's the most widely known form of a signature talk, but most crucially, the constraints of the form—the time limit, the prohibition on notes or podiums, the need to connect with both a live and digital audience—make the architecture of a great speech visible. When you understand how a TEDx talk works, you understand how all speeches work. The elements we'll explore—from attention-getters to calls to action—become clearer when we see them operating within these constraints.

The 30- to 60-second TEDx YouTube Shorts created from the talks often get more views than the full length talks. The same can be true for short clips that the speakers post on their personal social media pages. Another important difference between the TEDx talk and the keynote is there are no notes or podiums on the TEDx stage. You are up on the red dot, alone, and even the most practiced public speaker tends not to have a lot of practice doing *that*.

Perhaps most importantly, what you need to remember is that the audience for a TEDx talk is completely different than a keynote speech. The keynote is usually delivered for a specific audience that is there, live, right in front of you, whereas the primary audience for a TEDx talk is a digital global audience that extends well into the future—it's the internet.

While a TEDx talk *does* take place at a specific place and time, and with the help and support of local organizers, the moment when you give your TEDx talk is the moment when your audience is smallest. What you're really doing with your TEDx talk is creating a digital artifact which everyone everywhere will be able to access all the time. It's one of the things that people will find first when they google you. Therefore, it's written with *that* in mind, a talk with a reach and relevance that far exceeds the present moment, to maximize the potential for a universal audience to see themselves in it and take action.

One last thing—some chapters in this book are significantly longer than others. The reason for this is simple but important—this book follows the same structure we use for speeches. The lengthy chapters on building problems and presenting solutions mirror the expanded time these elements need in an actual speech. The shorter, punchier chapters on opening statements and calls to action reflect how these moments work best: brief, focused, and sharp.

We made this choice deliberately, even though it breaks some conventional rules about book structure. Just as we tell our clients that every element of their speech should serve a purpose, every chapter length in this book is intentional. When you need deep discussion and examples—like in exploring how to establish credibility or develop solutions—we take our time. When you need clarity and impact—like in crafting an attention-getter or call to action—we get straight to the point.

Consider this book an example of what we're teaching. As you read, you're not just learning about speech structure—you're experiencing it. The pacing, the development of ideas, the build-up of evidence and examples, even this moment of explaining what we're doing—it's all part of showing you how a great speech works from the inside out. Because the best way to learn something is to live it while you're learning about it.

Who Are You Guys Anyway?

If you've got *this* far in the book—if you've got the book at all—you might be wondering about *us*. You might be wondering about the origin story, the details, the when and the how, the what, the times and places, the circumstances that had to come together in order to create this book you hold in your hands. Or you might not give a flip, and that's okay too; feel free to skip ahead.

Cesar's speaking career began on a grade school cafeteria stage, where his cowboy-inspired delivery of a pilgrim's line at the first Thanksgiving unexpectedly brought the house down. This early success led him through the ranks of stand-up comedy, from military comedy tours in war zones to a Comedy Central appearance and a few roles in movies.

But even as his career seemed to be taking off in LA, Cesar felt increasingly disconnected from his audiences, prompting a pivot back to graduate school, where he studied creative writing and began teaching comedy classes in the theater department at a small liberal arts college. It was a shift that rekindled his passion for the stage and eventually led to a career as a speaker and a global TEDx speaker coach and keynote speechwriter.

During this time, Cesar's path intersected with Steve's, a tenured professor of English with a background in theater and public speaking. Steve was an English major from the start and had completed a doctorate in Shakespeare when his first book of fiction came out. He changed direction, putting his Shakespeare research on the backburner and concentrated on fiction and journalism.

Four books later—now a nationally bestselling author—he shifted focus yet again and wrote and directed an award-winning documentary feature. He and Cesar kept in close contact, and the two kept trying to find reasons and ways to collaborate.

Along the way, there were a number of versions of the work we're doing now—courses taught together, a podcast that fizzled out, and a regular radio show segment about a disgruntled movie critic that should have won an Emmy.

But this is different. This is more than a creative project. It's a way to lift others up, bring important messages to life, launch careers and businesses, and contribute to making the world better.

Really.

As many times as we've done it, as practiced as we've become in working in the various forms—the keynote speech, the TEDx talk, the corporate presentation, the brand story—there's always the same flash of excitement when we sit down with a client for the first time and they start telling us about their idea.

Everyone is different. Sometimes, our clients have just the start of an idea and want to flesh it out. Sometimes they have gone through a life-altering experience and want to share what they've learned with others. And sometimes they're Harvard-trained doctors, Olympic athletes, and professionals who have written a book and watched that book moldering on the shelf or refreshed their Amazon author page endlessly in the hopes that it would magically start selling. Either way, they've come to the conclusion that speaking is the way to bring their message to life.

"What's the gift you want to give your audience?" is how we start.

Then, we get to work. To bring their idea—their message—to life and to the stage.

There's nothing better.

CHAPTER ONE

The Blueprint

There's a difference between giving a speech and creating one.

The most accomplished, most often booked speakers *might* give the same keynote 30–60 times a year, or else have two or three different keynotes, versions of which they deliver depending on the circumstance.

These folks typically describe themselves as "seasoned public speakers." Which they are—they get up on stage *a lot*, are confident, and probably make a fair living giving speeches. They know a great deal about speaking, but it's not the same as what we do. We're in the speech kitchen every day, cooking up new ones. There's no actual speech kitchen, and there are no aprons involved, but you get the idea. When you're helping craft multiple speeches per week, patterns emerge. Solutions crystallize.

We didn't get here overnight. When the two of us first started giving talks ourselves—early in our own speaking careers—we thought what everyone else does, that it was all about the idea. Get a great idea, write it down, deliver it with passion—and boom, a standing ovation. Great ideas, we thought, speak for themselves.

It should be that simple, but it isn't.

A great idea is great, but what matters—what *really* matters—is structure. It's not the sexy part of speechwriting, not necessarily the first thing that people want to focus on when they make the leap onto the stage. And we get it. There are a lot of other things that seem like they should take priority, like what to do with your hands, or what to wear, or if your jokes are going to land, or how to deal with it if you suddenly start sweating. We've got advice for all of it, but it's not where we *start*.

Here's the truth: without the right structure, even the most brilliant idea will fall flat. We've seen it happen. *You've* seen it happen. Maybe it's happened to you. A speaker comes to us with an amazing concept, something that could, that should, genuinely change lives. They've got the credentials. They've got the passion. They've even got charisma. But their speech? It meanders. It circles. It never quite lands. Why? Because they're missing solid structure.

So, here's the blueprint: a great speech has seven—that's right, *seven*, there's an actual number—key ingredients. They're not random. They're not arbitrary. They're the result of years of trial and error, of finding what works and what doesn't, of helping speakers build talks from scratch or to transform okay talks into unforgettable ones.

We're going to get into each of them in depth and in detail in the rest of the book, but we're going to say what they are right away, hand them over, up front and without any suspense, so you can refer back to them whenever you need to. So there's no mystery. Keep in mind that not all speeches will follow this exact flow. As you become more experienced, you'll be able to play with these ingredients, reveal them in different ways, and perhaps, even break the blueprint altogether.

But for now, as the Mandalorian would say, "This is the way":

1. **Attention-Getter**

   Start with a **compelling attention-getter** that grabs your audience right from the start. This could be a story, a startling statement, or a question that gets the audience thinking. Think of it as your speech's first move. It needs to be bold, or funny, or both, at least *somewhat* unexpected, and most of all, it needs to build common ground with your audience. That common ground is crucial. It's the moment when your audience moves from just receiving the talk to actively engaging with it, when they're not just listening but relating, when *they* get that *you* get it. Whether you're sharing a personal anecdote, dropping a mind-blowing statistic that challenges preconceptions, or posing a question, your intro has got to do one thing and one thing only: get your audience to wonder what you're going to say *next*.

2. **Problem Statement**

   The second ingredient is a **clear problem statement** that lays out what's at stake. This is where you make it clear why what you're talking about matters and why the audience should care. It's not enough to simply state a problem—its weight and urgency have to be clear. What happens if we don't know about it or do nothing?

Try finishing this sentence: "The problem is _____." Being able to do this is crucial.

3. **Throughline**

    Third is the **throughline**—a succinct statement, one or two sentences long, that takes your idea and sets it in motion, moving your audience from where they are to where you want them to go. One way to shape the throughline is like this: "We need to stop doing X and start doing Y." This is the core argument of your speech, not just boiled down to its essence but communicated in terms of *change*. It's a powerful tool for keeping you and your audience focused on both the problem and the solution.

4. **Build the Problem**

    Step 4 is **building the problem,** whether it's using stats, research, personal stories, or whatever else might create urgency or need. This is where you really drive home why your idea matters and why we need to act now. It's also the place where you establish, or build, your *credibility* on the subject. This is your chance to showcase both why the problem demands attention and your unique perspective on solving it. Ideally, the evidence should be a mix of hard facts, stats, and story—most effective speakers blend statistics and research with personal stories, using data to establish scope and storytelling to build trust and credibility.

5. **Solutions**

    The fifth ingredient is **a clear vision of a concrete, actionable solution** the audience can actually implement. This can be a single, powerful step for the audience to take or a set of specific but related solutions that address the problem you've outlined. Whatever your approach, this part of the speech needs to be specific, practical, personal, and achievable. Avoid platitudes and too much complexity, and remember, your goal is to empower your audience, to help them feel that they can do something or that something can (and should) be done—helping us see how the world could be different and our role in that change.

6. **OMG Moment**

    Sixth is the OMG moment—the climax of your speech that takes it from great to unforgettable. So, what does it stand for? Oh, My God? Nay, Oh, My Gift! It's the twist, the revelation, the mic-drop moment that flips their expectations upside down, bringing everything full circle to what you're *giving* your audience. The deeper takeaway lingers long after the applause fades; the hidden thread ties everything together in a way that feels both shocking and inevitable.

    Nail this moment, and you're not just bringing your speech to its peak—you're rewriting how your audience sees everything that came before.

    This is where you reveal the real reason you're on that stage. Not your bio or your credentials, but the truth that made this idea impossible for you to ignore. It's most often a story, but it could also be a prop that's been hiding in plain sight or a revelation that shifts everything into focus.

    The key is that it has to be both **unexpected** and **earned**. When you deliver it right, your audience members won't just remember it—they'll be dying to tell someone else about it the second they walk out of the room.

7. **Call to Action**

    The seventh and final ingredient is **a call to action**. Be specific about what you want your audience to do, and make it as easy as possible for them to take that first step. End with a vision of what could be if everyone in the room (or on the internet) takes action—help your audience see themselves and your speech as part of something bigger, something transformative.

*NOTE: Depending on the kind of speech you're giving, numbers six and seven can swap places. For example: a TEDx talk will typically follow the flow above because it's a form where the call to action is central to the **idea**, whereas a keynote may have a more practical call to action like, "Use this QR code to donate now," in which case you wouldn't want to end there, wouldn't want it to be the very last thing you say. Instead, you'd want to bring them back to the story, to end on the strongest possible note, and have that resonate with the audience as they think back on what you said, on your idea, and the journey the talk took them on. Whether it's a sentence or a speech, people tend to most remember the last thing they hear.*

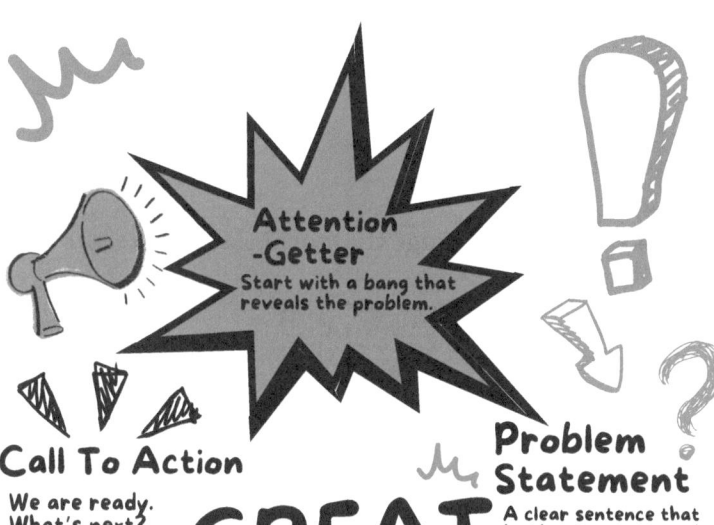

Attention-Getter
Start with a bang that reveals the problem.

GREAT SPEECH!
(The Blueprint)™

Call To Action
We are ready. What's next? How do we solve this problem together?

Problem Statement
A clear sentence that builds common ground but also challenges the status quo.

OMG Moment
Full circle moment. Reveal to us the emotional aha that ties it all together.

Throughline
The sentence that encapsulates your talk. Take us from where we are to where we could be.

Solution(s)
Your secret sauce. Your IP. Your idea. The transformation that's possible.

Build Problem
Agitate. Big. Urgent. Answer: Why now? Why you?

Great Speech!

Welcome to your first assignment!

Use the QR code below to download the fill in the blank blueprint now and complete it as you go through this book. You won't regret it.

A great speech can change the world. *Let's create yours.*

CHAPTER TWO

Attention-Getter

The first email we exchanged was three words long. Steve emailed Cesar in the middle of an opening speech they had both tuned out of and said: "I'm so bored."

This is a book about how to write and deliver speeches that won't bore anyone, speeches people will not just want to listen to but will actually share with others. And that's the first lesson: don't start in a way that makes the audience tune out and wish they were somewhere else. Anywhere else.

We're going to come back to this, but for now what you need to know is that we were stuck having to listen to a speech introducing a committee that we were both going to be sitting on—and it felt to us like it was never going to end.

Who knows what they were saying. We actually have no recollection.

We were that bored.

You might be wondering why we started the chapter this way. Why begin with boredom when we could have opened with something more dramatic—a standing ovation, a mic drop?

Because that's exactly how most speeches go wrong. They start with the wrong thing—with credentials, with context, with throat-clearing. They start everywhere *except* the one place they should: with something that makes the audience lean in.

We all know that beginnings matter, but the truth is that they matter more than you think. There are studies out there saying exactly this, that no audience has ever *started* suddenly to listen to a speech around minute eight, but we're not going to cite any of them. Because, well, it's that obvious.

Think about how you're reading this book right now. You didn't start on page 57. You didn't skip ahead to the chapter on solutions. You started at the beginning—because beginnings matter. But more than that, you kept reading past that story because you could connect to that moment—sitting there while someone gives a speech that makes you question every life choice that led you to that chair. Stuck in an audience.

We've all been there, watching a speaker who seems determined to test the limits of human attention, wondering how a subject so important, a topic that they clearly know a ton about, and *care* about, could be made so monumentally dull.

Maybe you kept reading because you saw hope—that there might be a way to make speeches not just worth listening to, but truly transformative. Or maybe it was just the audacity of two people who decided to turn their shared misery into a mission. In other words, you could *relate*.

Which is crucial in an opening. You want your audience to connect with you in some kind of way that's more than just intellectual. They need to *feel* it. Great talks are given by people we feel connected to who ask right or new questions about problems and situations we've experienced ourselves, or at least can see from a shared perspective.

Attention-Getter

We started with that story because we wanted to create a bond between speaker and audience. It says, "We've been where you are. We know what it's like ... and this blueprint is the way out." And so that's the scene with which we begin, with the two of us trapped in a room listening to a bad speech.

We *know* you can relate because bad speeches are everywhere. They happen all the time. For as long as there have been people, one of them has taken it upon themselves to stand up and give a speech, and most of those speeches have been mediocre, if not outright terrible. That's because speeches are *inherently* boring. If right now you're thinking about the last speech you gave and you're wondering, *was my speech really that boring?* We can, with near certainty and with kindness, say we fell asleep just thinking about it.

Don't take it personally. Even the people who *should* excel at it—folks with amazing minds who have amazing insights into important things—struggle with it. Think about your favorite subject in school. Maybe it was history, or biology, or literature. Now think about the teacher or professor who taught it.

Chances are you had that *one* teacher who knew everything there was to know about their particular area, who lived and breathed it, who *loved* it and wanted *you* to love it, who had dedicated their entire life to understanding and sharing it—and who *still* somehow managed to bore you to tears. They weren't bad teachers. They weren't uninformed or unprepared. They were experts. That was the problem. The more you know about something, the harder it is to make it interesting to others.

If you've spent decades becoming an expert in your field, if you understand all the nuances, all the complexities, it *doesn't* make it easier to engage other people on the subject.

It actually makes it more difficult. When you stand up to share that expertise, something goes wrong. Your audience's eyes glaze over. They start checking their phones. They're thinking about what they're going to have for lunch. Maybe actually leaving for lunch. Expertise just gets in the way of engagement. It's easy to forget that *you're* the one in the room most into what you have to say about your subject.

That's why some of the most distinguished and brilliant professors can clear a lecture hall faster than a fire alarm, and why some industry leaders can turn a roomful of eager listeners into a sea of yawns. The good news is this is fixable. But first, you have to accept that knowledge alone isn't enough. Expertise isn't enough. Even passion isn't enough. You need something else. This might be something you know intuitively, but if you've ever stood up in front of a group and delivered a talk, it's something that you've seen in the faces of your audience—they look at you as if to say they're ready for you to bore them *again*.

But it's not just speeches.

Everything is boring. And it isn't new—we've been perfecting the art of boring presentations since we first developed the ability to speak, and probably even before that. It's like something in our DNA compels us to take interesting things and make them tedious.

Before there were boring keynotes, there were boring startup pitch decks. Before that, boring sales conferences and boring meetings led by boring people. Before that, boring town hall meetings. Before that, boring royal proclamations. Before that, boring medieval tales about boring pilgrims. Before that, boring Romans asking you to lend them your ears. And before that, boring cave presentations where our ancestors literally bored each other to death with extremely

Attention-Getter

well-researched, detailed, and boring explanations of their wall paintings.

Some things never change. It is a sad but unavoidable truth that everything is *not* awesome. The good stuff of the universe is not sending out advertisements for itself. It doesn't even have an Instagram account. It's not even trying.

And these days, boredom has become particularly painful because we're never more than a few seconds away from something that's not just more entertaining, but *addictively* so. Our devices have trained us to expect continual and constant stimulation, cat videos, Amazon, Ebay, and TikTok.

You can see it happening in real time during speeches—that moment when you've lost them, when the audience starts to drift. They try to be polite about it at first. They maintain eye contact, but their minds are elsewhere. Then the phones come out, held low in their laps as if speakers can't tell what's happening.

Pro tip: we can tell. Nobody naturally stares at their crotch with that much interest and concentration.

But here's the thing: it's not phones that are the problem. They're just the current version of something that's always been true. Human beings are built to look for what matters, what's interesting, what's worth paying attention to. When we don't find it, we look elsewhere.

The ways of escape have changed, but the impulse hasn't. The universe doesn't care if we're entertained. Stars explode whether anyone's watching or not. That's where human beings come in—it's up to us to make everything interesting. From the most celebrated achievements of literature, to groundbreaking scientific insights, to the salad you decided *not* to order for lunch, everything that is interesting, or cool, or compelling is that way because some human being turned it into that.

Great Speech!

The speech we were listening to that day was *not* that kind of speech. But it could have been—it was a speech about how we were going to create a new logo.

Which does at least sound like it *could* be interesting.

The two of us were in the room for the first meeting of something called the "Logo Committee." Back then, we were both working at the same college, and that college had come to the conclusion that what was needed, with some degree of urgency, was a new logo.

The current logo was okay, but the college wanted something better. A logo that would take us into the next century, boldly, somewhere no college had been before. You get the idea. As is often the case in higher education, the next thing the college did after it made the decision to *do* something was to form a committee. And we were put on it.

As for *how* we got on that committee, it was not a mystery. The two of us were two moderately interesting people who happened to be employed by the college at that moment in history. And we weren't the only ones.

The room was filled with moderately to highly interesting people employed by the college, an assemblage of characters who, on paper, plausibly added up to exactly the right team to assemble if you wanted to come up with a logo.

There was an award-winning documentarian, a cool dude who worked in fundraising who wore mirrored sunglasses and a bow tie, a composer, the woman who had completely revamped the IT Department at the college a few years before and was an expert on computer hacking, and some guy from the Athletic Department who'd been in the NHL in the 90s and carried around an actual hockey card of himself along next to his driver's license. It *was* an interesting group. In fact, we were probably the two *least* interesting people in it.

But none of us had ever created a logo before.

The college had hired a logo firm to produce the actual logo, of course. They were the experts, but it was clear right from the start that *we* were the ones responsible. We were steering the ship. The logo people knew logos, but *we* knew the place and the people, the history and the mission—the brand—of the college.

This made total sense to everyone involved. They had been on campus for forty-five minutes, while one of our fellow interesting committee members had worked there for longer than either of us had been alive. We were an *essential* part of the process. They told us that, and we believed it. Entirely. It was *our* job to come up with something that would capture fully what was important about the place, but more than that, we needed to do so in a fresh and unique way and to put it all into a logo that would forever and ever, or at least for the next ten years, sit atop everything from stationary to the hockey arena.

At first, the fact that we had exactly zero logo experience didn't matter. It even seemed as if it might *help*. Had you asked us if prior experience in logo construction was something we needed, most of us would have told you "No!" This was a vague feeling during that first meeting, but it gained momentum the more meetings we had, the more we sat there brainstorming—which is what committees always do when they start working together and have a totally unclear idea of what they are supposed to be doing.

We talked about the logos in our lives, what we liked and didn't like, what we *loved* about them. We looked at some examples of great and not-so-great logos, and then more logos that seemed like knock-offs of other logos. We checked out logos of other colleges and looked at mascots—there are a *lot* of tigers—and then went over the long history of the logos of our own college, at the way our own logo had transformed and then transformed again over the last century and a half.

Which is when it happened: the more we talked, the more we wondered if maybe we were, somehow, surprisingly, logo experts. We all knew what a logo was, we realized, and we'd not just seen a few logos, we had seen a *lot*.

There was a kind of energy in the room. Any skepticism that any of us might have had vanished. This was going to be awesome. Our logo was going to be awesome. Maybe the freshness of our perspective was exactly what the logo business had been lacking up to that point when our committee was formed. Maybe this was going to be the logo committee that would blow the whole logo creation industry wide open.

We could not have been more mistaken. And this is a mistake—*the* mistake— most people make with *speeches* all the time. We think anyone who *can* talk can *give* a talk. It's actually more than just something that we think, it's something we act on. You'd never look out at the crowd gathered for your wedding and ask your second cousin—a guy who can't even whistle—to come up and take over for the guitarist in the band.

But when it comes to giving a speech, we do it all the time. This is the world we live in: it's a truth universally acknowledged that no matter how much we love or hate public speaking, we *all* will be asked to give a speech at some point, regardless of whether or not we have any experience.

It's for that reason so many of us find ourselves pulled up onstage, thrust into the spotlight, expected to deliver words of wisdom, hilarious (and appropriate) jokes, deep insights, absorbing anecdotes, the whole shebang, with zero preparation. This happens perhaps most often at weddings, but it's not just weddings. It's retirement parties, corporate events, community gatherings, town hall meetings—the list is long.

What makes things worse for both the speaker and the audience is we don't get a support team for these impromptu moments when someone hands us the mic. There's no speechwriter, no equivalent of the logo design team working with us to help craft the thing, no coach helping us nail our delivery.

We're out there on our own, armed with nothing but an unclear and likely deeply flawed idea of what we're supposed to say and the hope that we won't make fools of ourselves.

At best, we give a speech everyone forgets, and at worst, it's painful and embarrassing. We remember the speech for years. And not in a good way. The way to avoid that is by starting with an opening statement and getting the audience on your side.

As we've said, it's good if you can get them interested, and it's better if you can get them to *relate*. The talks we remember, the ones that stick with us, the speeches that remain vivid years later aren't just smart. They're smart, but they're not only smart, they *also* hit us in the gut, make us feel something.

It's like that old story about the elephant and the rider. You can talk the rider into doing *almost* anything, and *sometimes,* the elephant will do what the rider tells it to do. But not all the time. Once the elephant starts to move, on the other hand, once it makes up its mind that it's going in a particular direction, that it's going to take action, the rider can't do much to stop it.

That's what emotional connection is like, it's the most primitive, most irrational, most unstoppable side of the brain, and that's why it's crucial to appeal to it along with the rational side of your audience. Your emotions are the elephant in the room, and though it might be a mistake to speak only to it, or to it first, we forget it, or ignore it, at our peril.

So what about your opening statement? Your attention-getter. It sounds important because it is important, but how do you find one? Here are a few places to start.

1. Think about the moments when you've **already got people excited about your topic**—maybe it's a LinkedIn post that got unexpected traction, or an analogy you use that always lands, or even just the way you explain what you do at parties that makes people lean in and ask questions. You probably already have a killer opening statement; you just don't know it yet. That story you tell all the time because you know it gets people into it. That one thing you say that makes the person you're talking to say they've never thought of it like that before. Chances are, hidden in one of those is the perfect way to open your speech—a proven way to connect and get the attention of your audience that you've already road-tested in the real world.

2. Another thing to try is to **write three opening statements that *could* start your speech**. The first should be informational—just the facts. The second should be centered around making your audience curious—give them a reason to wonder what comes next. The third should aim at creating an emotional connection, showing your audience that you understand them. Now, ask yourself which one, or which combination of them, seems most engaging. It's usually the case that you can tell which is most interesting because *you're* most interested in it, that the experience of hearing yourself say your potential opening

Attention-Getter

statements out loud tells you a lot about how other folks will experience them.

3. If your topic is something that you've written a lot about—maybe a dissertation, or some piece of original research—**try explaining it to someone who knows nothing about it in plain language.** Imagine you're having coffee with a friend and they ask about your idea. Just tell them. Don't pull up any notes or a slide deck, don't read from anything. Say it out loud and record yourself doing it. Maybe actually do this with someone, maybe even while drinking coffee. If they ask questions, answer them. Explain the parts they don't get. Say why it matters. Notice how you connect the topic to their experience, how you build common ground without even thinking about it. That's the voice you want in your opening statement. That's how you want to start.

Here's your second assignment!

Write a question, a startling statement, or a quick story that grabs attention immediately. Remember, craft an opening that would make YOU lean in, but also builds common ground.

If you haven't downloaded the fill in the blank great speech blueprint, here it is again:

CHAPTER THREE

Problem Statement

We all have a tendency to overestimate our understanding of a creative form when we've seen or experienced it. **We mistake experience for expertise.**

It's a peculiarly human trait, this bias towards confidence, the confidence that watching something translates into knowing how to create it. We see it everywhere: in the sports fan who's certain they could coach better than the coach, or the driver in the backseat who is always willing to offer feedback. (This is, by the way, not something that either of us have done. Ever. Not once in our lives.)

This confidence isn't entirely misplaced—experience *does* teach us something. Watch enough baseball games, and you'll end up knowing something about why you want to keep the runner at second base. Watch enough movies, and you'll have a pretty clear idea of why a director went for a closeup at a decisive moment, but there's a difference between understanding how something works and being able to do it yourself. Between recognizing quality and being able to produce it.

This problem becomes acute when we move from passive observation to active creation. That's when we discover that all those hours of watching and experiencing *haven't* prepared us for the actual work of creating something ourselves.

The first sentence of this chapter? That's the problem statement of this book. And like all good problem statements, it contains within it the seed of its own solution.

The problem is that we have a tendency to overestimate our understanding of what makes a great speech because we've seen so many speeches. We mistake *experience* **for** *expertise***.**

Now, we know that's *not* all of you. And by "you" we mean, well, "you," the person who is actually reading this book. You're probably *not* overconfident about speaking—you're tentative, maybe terrified. Your palms might perspire just thinking about getting up in front of people. Which is, in fact, what *most* people are like.

Maybe that's you. Maybe you're here because you've just been asked to give a speech and the idea is freaking you out. We see you. And you're in the right place. You've seen others make this mistake, and you're not making it yourself. You're actually doing the work to get this right.

But it was *definitely* a problem that day in the logo committee in those first meetings, where we all started to think that maybe, just maybe, we were the logo committee to end all logo committees, win the gold, and possibly set the world record. We didn't know if there *was* a world record for logos, but if there was, we might just be in contention for it.

The fact that we knew next to nothing about the form seemed a distinct advantage. Only it wasn't. And it never is, but unlike creating a logo, most of us carry around the idea that a speech *should* be the sort of thing anyone can just do.

That's how it's different from designing a logo, and had it not been for that first flush of overconfidence and excitement, we would have, or should have, seen that ourselves because the truth is that there was something a little strange about being appointed to a logo committee in the first place. For most of us—for most human beings—designing a logo is a new thing.

No one gets up and gives a logo at their daughter's wedding. No one has even seen anyone do that. Or try to.

No coach has ever walked into the locker room at halftime, down by two touchdowns, and thought to themselves: "It's my job to come up with an inspiring logo."

No one is asked to get up in front of her class in fourth grade and deliver a logo about reptiles.

Logo design was not just something we had never done before; it was something most of us had never even *thought* about doing. All the same, the question we eventually found ourselves asking was exactly what people ask when they're asked to give a speech despite having no clear idea about how to do it: *how hard can it be?* The logo pros were *not* thinking the same thing. They knew it was going to be hard. That it would mean work. That there was trial and error and expertise involved.

They also knew it was important.

Regardless of how much you might hate or love the idea of a logo, you know they matter. That was us—it didn't matter how skeptical any of us were at the start of things, we were united in believing that work on the logo was work worth doing. Maybe it was not entirely clear what particular improvement a good logo would bring to the college as a

Problem Statement

whole, but a bad logo—one that was ridiculous—would be a disaster.

Looking back over the history of logos at the college, it was clear that mistakes had been made. The idea was to avoid making another. It was for that reason the college had put so much time into assembling a bunch of interesting people and telling them to come up with something captivating, innovative, intelligent, unique and, yes, interesting.

They needed a logo for the ages, one that contained the essence of the adventure students would embark upon when they choose to come to our college. The idea behind the committee, in short, was a good one. Sure, it was obviously a mistake, but it was a mistake that made *sense*. We knew about the college a lot—we didn't just work there but had made it part of our lives. If anyone was going to make a great logo, it would be subject matter experts like us.

That's a mistake we see a lot when it comes to writing speeches. With a few conspicuous exceptions, the one thing that unites all of our clients—and all speakers—is their *connection* to their subject matter. They know their stuff. Usually that's the reason they're giving the speech in the first place.

TEDx talks and keynote speeches are clear examples of where it's crucial to establish credibility—but it's true of all speeches. That fourth grader up there presenting on the Gila monster has literally taken out all the books in the school library about reptiles. The bridesmaid giving a speech at her best friend's wedding is a subject matter expert.

Which is exactly right. If you have a message, if you believe you have something to say that needs to be *heard*, you need to be on a stage speaking. This is a valid and excellent impulse. The *mistake* is thinking your expertise, the specific knowledge you have or the insight you've gained through experience, translates into the ability to write and deliver an effective speech about it.

That was the mistake that all of us on the logo committee made. We were all interesting and creative people, and we all had made interesting and creative things. Just not a logo. When it comes to speeches, there are any number of wrong turns that people make.

Maybe their speech is primarily a story about them, or maybe they believe they're better (more themselves, more authentic, more spontaneous) when they just wing it, or they do the opposite and just read from their script or, worse, the book they wrote years before. In all of these cases the result is a disengaged audience and a speaker who leaves the stage feeling deflated and ineffective.

The fundamental challenge, we've found, isn't getting people to recognize that they need help with their speeches—most of our clients come to us knowing that much. The challenge is getting them to step back from their solutions long enough to clearly articulate the *problem* they're trying to solve.

It's like they've skipped ahead to the answer without fully understanding the question. Brilliant people come to us with PowerPoint decks full of data, with personal stories they're sure will move audiences, with the most stirring, most urgent calls to action that you can imagine.

What they *don't* have is a clear statement of the problem their talk is meant to address. When we ask them to complete the simple sentence "The problem is …" they struggle. Not because they don't know their subject, not because they don't think there's a problem—they know it inside and out—but because the"re so deep inside their expertise and the subject that they've lost sight of why it matters to anyone else.

Problem Statement

This is where the *form* of a speech becomes crucial. Unlike a research paper or a technical presentation, a great speech isn't fundamentally about handing over information. It's not a download. It's about creating a *bridge* between your expertise and their experience. And that bridge always, always starts with a clear problem statement. Not a solution, not a set of credentials—a problem that the audience can recognize and relate to.

Your audience doesn't care about your expertise until they understand *why* they should. They don't care about your solutions until they feel the weight of the problem. And they certainly don't care about your personal journey until they see how it connects to their own.

That's why we spend so much time with our clients on problem statements. It might sound too simple to be true, but the way we get them onto the common ground, which will allow them to convey their idea effectively and directly to an audience (any audience), is to get them to complete this sentence:

"The problem is ... "

That's a problem statement. And note, when we talk about problem statements, we're not talking about gentle suggestions or subtle hints. These are sentences that land with the force of recognition. Statements that make people stop, look up, and think, "Finally, someone is saying it."

Think about Chimamanda Ngozi Adichie's statement that "The problem with gender is that it prescribes how we should be rather than recognizing how we are." Or Angela Duckworth's "Our potential is one thing. What we do with it is quite another." When Brené Brown says, "You can have courage or you can have comfort, but you cannot have both," *that's* a problem statement.

These aren't warm-ups to the real message. They're not context-setting or scene-setting. They are the problem, stripped down to its essence and delivered with unmistakable clarity.

The best problem statements have an inevitable quality to them—once you hear them, you can't unhear them. They change how you see the world. When Bill Gates stepped onto the TED stage and said, "The world today has 6.8 billion people ... that's headed up to about 9 billion. Now, if we do a really great job on new vaccines, health care, reproductive health services, we could lower that by perhaps 10 or 15 percent," he wasn't telling a story about his foundation's work, he was stating a problem that *demanded* attention.

This is what we mean when we say your problem statement should not be mistaken for something else. It's not background information. It's not a personal anecdote. It's not a call to action. It's the moment in your speech when you point to the elephant in the room. And call it an elephant. When you say the thing that everyone knows but no one has been willing or able to articulate. Everything else in your speech—your stories, your expertise, your solutions—flows from this moment of clarity.

It's not as easy as it seems. But once you've done it, once you've identified the core of the issue that you're seeking to solve, you've made real progress.

Try it yourself, with that idea that you have been kicking around for what feels like forever but has never quite made it onto the page, or the stage, or out of your head, just fill in the blank:

The problem is _____.

Problem Statement

Don't rush it. Don't try to sound smart or sophisticated. Don't worry about whether it's TEDx-worthy or keynote-ready. Just complete the sentence. Then, complete it again. And again. Keep going until you find the version that makes you sit up straighter, that makes your pulse quicken slightly, that makes you think, "Yes, that's exactly it." The version that doesn't just describe what's wrong but captures why it matters.

Assignment #3:

Craft YOUR problem statement. What's the problem that's keeping you up at night? What's that one thing no one's talking about but should? Now, complete this sentence:

"The problem is …"

Or maybe the problem is that you haven't downloaded the blueprint yet? Now that's easily solved. Find it here:

CHAPTER FOUR

Throughline

> *If you can't write your message in a sentence,
> you can't say it in an hour.*
>
> —Dianna Booher

S**tep one:** Start off your speech by coming out strong with a statement that grabs the audience and makes them want to listen—to *actively* wonder what you're going to say next.

Step two: Complete this sentence: The problem is_____.

Now to step three: The "throughline."

If you've never heard of a "throughline," it's a term used a lot by screenwriters, though it's going to be familiar to anyone who is working in media, and also to people in sales—in any sector, basically, where *story* is crucial. We're not using the word "throughline" in an identical manner to any of those, but it's not unrelated.

For us and when it comes to speeches, the throughline is the thread that holds a talk together, and it's centered on an idea in a way that conveys *motion*. It's not just a point A and a point B, but the *journey* from one to another. The throughline both tells you where you *started* and where you're *going*. It's the driving force behind the plot of a movie in the same way it drives a keynote or a TEDx talk.

Without it, your speech is in danger of becoming a series of disjointed anecdotes and facts. When your audience can't see a clear destination early in the talk, they begin to wonder if there is one. That leaves them lost and disengaged. And checking their phones.

Our emphasis on the throughline forms the core of our method, and it comes straight out of our experiences on the stage and page. When we decided to make the move into the work we're doing now, it made sense for us to build a framework based on the experience we already had in the media.

People sometimes find it strange to hear us talk about a speech's throughline, but it's crucial because it doesn't just clarify the idea—it sets it in motion. Getting people to think in terms of throughlines is a way of showing clients that speeches, like the best movies, novels, and jokes, as Nancy Duarte says in her TEDx talk, "Take the audience from where they are to where they could be."

Here's an example of a throughline we crafted for one of our clients:

We need to stop buying into the idea that we have nothing left to offer after a certain age and start seeing the fourth quarter of our lives as a time to redefine and reinvent ourselves.

What the throughline captures in the field of speechwriting is the sense of motion—how a speech should start in one place (such as a mistaken or misinformed understanding of a topic or issue) and end in another (the change in thinking, or in action, the speech is all about creating)

Here's another example from a client of ours:

Over two hundred thousand patients die each year in the US from preventable medical errors. If doctors take just two minutes to listen to their patients, millions of lives would be saved.

This is a great throughline. It starts with the same alarming statistic the speech itself begins with and elicits concern (sure, we know that medical error happens, but it's far worse than we thought), then provides an elegant and actionable solution (take two minutes to listen to patients).

When put into practice, what the throughline captures is the *form* of a speech. And that's what it's all about. Form is the tissue that holds a speech together and, as with most things having to do with communication, it's harder to see, but it's there.

That's why we get our clients to work with the throughline—it doesn't just give the speech form, it tells the audience what that form is. Your speech is your idea when spoken—and your form is the shape of that content. The sooner you can stop thinking of your idea and the process where you give it concrete shape as separate, the sooner you can get it out there in the world. The sooner other people can hear it.

Clients sometimes think of the throughline as a catchy phrase they're going to use for the title of their talk or as a type of thesis statement. And it is both of those things. Sort of.

But unlike a static thesis statement or a great title, a throughline is all about movement and progression. It's not just about what an idea is, but also about its evolution, where it started and where it's going. It takes us there. What's crucial is motion because the throughline not only conveys the essence of the idea but also its application and transformation. It's about connecting dots in a way that creates a path for understanding and action, making the idea not just clear, but also relatable and actionable.

In the movie *The Shawshank Redemption*, the throughline can be seen in the journey of the main character, Andy Dufresne, played by Tim Robbins. If you've never seen the movie, put this book down immediately and do precisely that.

Actually, do that *after* you've finished this book.

If you haven't seen it, here's the basics: Andy is a banker wrongly convicted of the murder of his wife and her lover, who is sent to Shawshank State Penitentiary (where the name of the movie comes from!). Despite prison being no picnic (to put it mildly), Andy maintains his dignity and hope, befriending fellow inmate Ellis "Red" Redding and others. Over the course of many years—this is the middle of the movie—he uses his financial expertise to help the corrupt warden and the prison guards. It's only at the end of the movie (spoiler alert) that Andy's plan unfolds as a brilliant escape he had been secretly orchestrating for years.

If you didn't see the escape coming, you weren't watching. In throughline terms, Robbins' character must "stop accepting a life of injustice and confinement" (X) and "start finding hope and freedom in the most unlikely places" (Y).

Here's the throughline of *this* book:

We need to stop ignoring and distrusting form and start prioritizing it as the backbone of your speech. Form is what allows meaning to emerge.

To say it again, the throughline is a statement with this shape: we need to stop doing X and start doing Y.

This isn't written in stone—there are many ways to shape a throughline—but this way effectively brings clarity to a speaker's thinking as well as the idea itself. It's a promise that they are going to get something out of your talk. If you can distill your idea into one sentence, with the first part challenging a status quo and the second proposing a clear, actionable solution, you're on your way.

Now for assignment #4:

It's your turn to complete your throughline. Fill in the blanks:

We need to stop doing _____ and start doing _____.

Take a few runs at it and see which one—or which combination—most clearly articulates where you're starting with your audience and where you want to take them.

You haven't downloaded the blueprint yet? Good Lord. Here you go:

CHAPTER FIVE

Build the Problem

The next step is to build and deepen the problem as well as to establish credibility for yourself as the speaker. The three primary questions you want to answer are:

1. **Why are you the person to help us solve this problem?**
2. **Why is it urgent that we solve this problem?**
3. **Why is now the time to solve this problem?**

There are countless ways of doing this, but we're going to focus on just a few ways to build a reliable, persuasive connection to the topic.

The most basic way to build a problem is through statistics. If a problem is a problem for a lot of people, then it must be an actual problem. Which is true, but we live in an age of data, and there is a lot of data out there. The fact is, too much data can cause your audience to turn off. It's probably the most common mistake we see.

Speakers will bombard the audience with an onslaught of numbers and percentages without context or narrative. Numbers are useful, but numbers alone are never going to be the foundation of a great talk. Statistics, studies, data, these are all supports for generating real engagement and investment from your audience, but not a replacement for it.

When you present a statistic, its relevance needs to be immediately clear and be a part of a larger story that you're telling. There is probably a lot of data out there to back up the claim that data is hard for folks to connect with, but we're not going to cite any of it. Because it'd make you tune out.

See what we did there? That was a data-driven joke about data, but it's also something that you know already. Think about your own experience, that feeling when a barrage of stats causes your brain to throw up its hands and walk out.

So, is there a non-mind-numbing way to use statistics? Here's an example from a client of ours we mentioned already. She's a surgeon who wanted to address the epidemic of medical misdiagnosis in the United States, and you've already seen the throughline of her speech about how medical error can be avoided by the simple step of doctors taking just two minutes to listen to their patients.

No question, this is an urgent and also serious, widespread problem, which means one of the challenges in bringing her talk to the stage was not *finding* evidence to back up the points she wanted to make but *deciding* which data to actually use. As you might imagine, she—a data-driven doctor—came in with a wide variety of alarming stats.

For example, an estimated 795,000 people in the US die or are permanently disabled each year due to misdiagnosis. About 3 in 4 of all misdiagnoses happen to people experiencing one of the so-called "Big Three": heart attack, infections,

Build the Problem

or cancer. On average, she told us, researchers estimate that 11 percent of medical problems result in a misdiagnosis.

No question, 795,000 people is a lot. But it's *too* big a number—it's so large it becomes not just impersonal and hard to grasp, but also something it feels like we can't do anything about. There's no connection to your experience or to anything real.

It also tends to get presented along with the health conditions that are associated with misdiagnosis, which are important, but which take away from the core of the idea. It's then that research on the topic tends to move into numbers that are actually very significant but *sound* small, like the 11 percent of medical problems that result in a misdiagnosis—the 11 percent represents hundreds of thousands of people, but it sounds like the opposite.

Here's how we helped her frame the problem so that it came across loud and clear:

> *The numbers are staggering—over two hundred thousand patients die each year in the US from medical mistakes. This is an epidemic of medical errors, the third leading cause of death in the US—doctor error results in our losing the equivalent of a jumbo jet crashing every single day. And while there are multiple factors at play, a key underlying issue is the erosion of trust and connection between physicians and patients. Studies show that, on average, doctors interrupt patients within just eleven seconds of them starting to speak—this means critical information is missed and misdiagnosis becomes far more likely.*

That's a stat you can *feel*. Eleven seconds is a small number that *sounds* small. Instead of using it to communicate the

magnitude of the problem, we're using it to show how little time doctors are spending with their patients.
She then followed it with a personal connection.

> *I say this as a doctor myself. I have been there. Overloaded with administrative tasks and glued to computer screens, we barely make eye contact, let alone give patients the space to share their full story. This pattern of disconnection has become normalized, but the consequences—the suffering, the lives lost—should not be seen by anyone as normal. It's a crisis hiding in plain sight.*

That's a problem that just became real—and then she made it more so by sharing a mistake that she herself almost made:

> *I'll never forget a patient, we'll call her Sarah, who came in with a host of unresolved symptoms. My first thought: I don't have time for this. But she made me listen to her entire story. As a result, I got crucial details that previous doctors had missed. That allowed me to diagnose a rare condition and swiftly get her the treatment she desperately needed.*

This small moment, this clear moment of insight, turned into a concrete and actionable solution that her fellow doctors—and patients—could apply:

> *Studies have shown that if they're not interrupted, most people take less than two minutes to say everything they have to say in a doctor's office. This is time we can afford, but how do we find it? It starts with changing medical education in a way that places listening and communication skills on par with technical expertise. It also means seeing that as doctors*

we have a responsibility to push back against a system where efficiency is king instead of quality of care.

Here's another example, this one from a client who is a professional musician and celebrated music teacher. She's a former winner of the World Accordion Championships and is now a judge for the same competition with a personal story that is both heartbreaking and inspiring.

The central idea of the talk she wanted to give was about reframing disability. She could have approached it through stats. For example, 12.1 percent of US adults have a mobility disability with serious difficulty walking or climbing stairs. That's a lot of people—12.1 percent of Americans are actually 40 million people. But 12.1 *sounds* small and almost shrinks the problem.

But that wasn't the real issue. The 12.1 percent is a number without a face, and the facelessness of that number was, in fact, the primary problem that the talk was going to address. So instead, we went in the other direction. We outlined the problem but then made it real through another emotional story she shared about how, after some remarkable early success in music, she almost stopped performing:

> *I was fifteen at the time and someone showed me a video of myself at an international accordion competition. I was horrified at the sight of myself walking across the stage with my crutches. Is that what I look like? What's wrong with me? Before then, that had been a question that other people had asked. Now, I was asking it myself and, for a time, I let it stop me. I stopped performing entirely. One day, a dear friend took me aside, and asked what was the matter. When I told her, she was confused. She said she had stopped seeing the crutches.*

Once again, when it comes to framing your problem, the primary questions you want to answer are:

1. **Why is now the time to solve this problem?**
2. **Why is it urgent that we solve this problem?**
3. **Why are you the person to help us solve this problem?**

So far, so good, but there's an intermediate step, and that's the deepening of the problem. This is crucial in any speech, as it ensures that the audience really gets what's at stake is the personal credibility and connection you have to your idea. This credibility-building moment—the why *you* moment of the talk—must occur in the *middle* of the speech and *not* at the start of it.

If this seems counterintuitive to you, you're not the only one. Many of our clients want to *start* with their credibility. We get it, and in some cases that's not a mistake, but a lot of the time it is precisely that.

If you happen to be, for example, the person who made some entirely incredible and unique discovery in the Amazon rainforest, and that's what your talk is about, start there. Most people are not that person. And even if you *are*, it might not be a bad idea to keep that close to your chest until exactly the right moment.

That's not because credibility isn't important—it's essential—but for it to function in the context of your talk, the audience needs to be able to understand why it's crucial. Credibility—or what we might call "credentialing"—can actually harm a talk if not presented in the right manner.

More on that in a moment.

The crucial thing to note here is while there are many ways to build credibility and make it clear why you are the right person to speak on your topic, explaining why it matters as a problem to you involves establishing your personal involvement in it. Though personal stories are pivotal in terms of the main two kinds of talks that we help clients bring to the stage—the keynote and the TEDx talk—they play a slightly different role in each.

One of the central misconceptions people have when they approach a TEDx talk is that it has mostly to do with personal story, that their talk should begin and end there, and that the rest of it—the idea, the problem, the solution, the call to action—is beside the point.

This is, in fact, the most common mistake that leads to TEDx talks *not* getting selected. They're heavy on personal stories and light on everything else. There should be no mystery or mistake about this—TEDx says it over and over in all of its communications. This is because they want to differentiate themselves from the world of motivational speaking where the focus is solely to inspire and motivate. It's easy to get this wrong because often, the part of a TED talk we remember most clearly is the personal story.

On the other hand, personal story and credibility are center stage when it comes to a keynote. The focus is on what you do and why your audience should engage with you in some way, be that to hire you or buy your book.

When we craft a keynote for a client, we're crafting the talk they are going to give whenever they are asked to present about what they do and how they do it. What stays central in the keynote is the client, their brand, and most of all the story of how they got to the moment when they got asked to be the keynote speaker for the event.

Great Speech!

But no matter what the kind of talk they're planning to give, a critical step in our process of working with all of our clients involves clarifying, elaborating, and in some cases *narrowing* their credibility to fit the topic of their talk and the problem it solves. This can be a personal connection, but neither credibility nor personal connection can stand on their own. In a truly compelling speech, they're combined and connected, and presented in a way that adds up to a coherent story.

While both keynotes and TEDx talks follow the same fundamental blueprint—attention-getter, problem statement, throughline, build the problem, solutions, OMG moment, call to action—they differ significantly in their endpoints.

A keynote typically will have its call to action—a clear pathway for the audience to work with you, learn from you, or otherwise benefit from your expertise, just before the end of the speech but not right at the end. This might mean a slide with a QR code to sign up for your email list, or following you on social media, buying your book, or simply connecting with you at the back of the room.

Your talk should naturally lead to this moment, making it feel less like a sales pitch and more like a logical, almost inevitable, next step in the journey you've shared. The very end, though, is typically an OMG moment story that ties all together, so that you're closing on an emotion rather than business.

TEDx talks, on the other hand, as we've said, must remain focused on the *idea*. TED's guidelines explicitly prohibit direct marketing or self-promotion. This doesn't mean you can't share personal stories—you absolutely should—but they need to serve the *idea* rather than build your brand.

Build the Problem

The call to action in a TEDx talk should inspire the audience to engage with the idea, not with you personally as a speaker, and that's why it can be placed at the very end of the talk. This might seem like a limitation, but it actually creates a powerful opportunity: if your idea resonates strongly enough, audience members will seek you out on their own.

This distinction affects how we shape the entire talk, particularly the later moments of it, such as the OMG moment and call to action (more on both of them in a few pages!). In a keynote, your personal transformation often becomes the model for what's possible, leading naturally to an invitation for the audience to work with you. In a TEDx talk, your personal story serves as evidence of the idea's power, building toward a call to action that focuses on implementing the idea itself, regardless of whether the audience ever connects with you personally.

To give just one example of *narrowing* credibility, a client of ours had switched from finance into tech at a relatively late age—she was in her forties—and was in the process of building a brand around navigating career transitions, whether that meant leaving a company or moving to a different role within the same organization. That was the central idea of her keynote and her credibility was that she had not just survived change but thrived from one big industry to the next.

She had practiced what she was now preaching. But, at the same time, she had also built a successful side business in real estate. Which was extremely interesting—and she had a lot to say about the topic—but it would have been a mistake to have her audience considering a side hustle buying and selling property when the heart of her talk was really about career transition. While there is a connection, ultimately the experience didn't link to her primary credibility with the problem and solution.

We encouraged her to leave that out of the talk. It was interesting, but it was a little *too* interesting.

Credibility is important, but in the context of a speech, it has to be *created* in a particular way. Which is *not* what happens in real life. When we go to the dentist, we want to see that DDS degree on the wall and not have to listen to the whole story of why the dentist wanted that degree in the first place. When you take your car in for an oil change, it would be weird if the mechanic told you about his first car, how he began repairing it, and how it led into the rest of his life.

But if your dentist was giving a *speech* about a new method he had created for filling teeth, and his audience knew nothing about him, it would be important and lend significantly to the credibility of the speech for him to get into all of it—maybe how he found his calling, the whole backstory of what drew him to dental school, the gleaming moment when he filled his first tooth and started to think, "Maybe there's a better way of doing this." The previous sentence is one that we never thought we'd have the chance to write.

Bottom line: in everything but speeches, expertise speaks for itself. In a speech, the opposite is true. Expertise has to have a backstory. Being an expert provides the foundation of knowledge and authority necessary to speak on a subject, but without a personal connection, your idea is distant or academic. A lived connection is the key to establishing real credibility. It really does make or break the speech.

Just as a moving and powerful personal connection between a speaker and her topic can transform it from good to great, a wrong step can sabotage it in a fundamental way. It's also what makes them enjoyable and shareable—we share a talk online because we want the person we're sharing it with to actually hear it. There's something crucial about

Build the Problem

that experience, the hearing and seeing it from the speaker themselves, that can't be conveyed by any summary.

Which is not to say it's easy to do. We've all been there, attending a work presentation, listening to a keynote, or watching a TEDx talk online when a well-intentioned (and also well-informed) speaker switches into a personal story in a way that goes wrong. Before we know it, something inside us switches off. Some reflex makes us think, at some level, "Who cares what else this guy has to say."

Don't be that person.

Here's how *not* to incorporate a personal story into your talk.

Not long ago in our review of emerging TEDx talks on YouTube, we came across one about a revolutionary organizational method the speaker developed, which significantly helps people manage stress (some details have been changed to protect the innocent). It was a simple, great idea, but he started with his credentials—not just the fact that he had attended an Ivy league school, but what made him focus on this particular topic and he did it by telling us a story that, you guessed it, featured him.

"I realized that existing organizational methods were inadequate," he said (not exactly that, but almost), "so, I single-handedly developed a groundbreaking technique. It was clear from the start that my approach was superior, everywhere I presented it, people were amazed at the degree and the depth to which it transformed their lives. It's now widely recognized as the best way to reduce stress."

There was then a moment of awkward silence.

"I have the numbers to prove it," he said.

And he did.

There was still no reaction from the audience. Instead there was the sound of the audience wondering how soon they could leave. The idea was brilliant, he was brilliant, and he had done the work. However, he positioned himself as the sole architect of a revolutionary method in his story. It was absolutely true, but it didn't matter; it hurt him. The idea was a great one, but the story was self-congratulatory, and all at once, it didn't matter how brilliant his brilliant idea was—no one got to the end of the talk.

This is why collaboration is so crucial. It's often the case that we're just too close to both our ideas and our personal story to judge them effectively; we lack the distance necessary to mold and to shape them into a speech.

We saw that very clearly in one of our favorite clients. He was a personal trainer who had developed an innovative fitness approach, leading to remarkable weight loss results. After working with him, we actually became his clients! We met him on Zoom, and even from the limited perspective afforded by our computer screens, it was plain to see that he was fit.

He himself was evidence of the effectiveness of the idea that he wanted to get onto the TEDx stage and deliver. Curiously, he *did* have a story of vulnerability in his past, back before he was the fitness guru he would later become. But instead of leading with the story, instead of turning there when it came to establishing his personal credibility, he focused on success metrics and his role as the architect of this method.

He said something like this:

"In my career as a personal trainer, I've devised a unique fitness regimen that consistently produces extraordinary results. Each client who has followed my method has lost a significant amount of weight, far surpassing the industry average."

Again, not a direct quote, but close.

Setting aside the fact that this approach would not have been successful as a TEDx talk because it would have been a direct advertisement for himself and his services—there was no hint of the personal journey behind the method, or that he had arrived at it because of everything he had been through.

Eventually, we got there, but it was only through asking a very direct question: "Did you ever struggle with your weight?"

"I nearly died," was his reply, and he seemed a little taken aback by the obviousness of the question. "I got into obesity management," he told us, "because I know what it's like to overcome obesity." It was an authentic connection between himself and his topic but he just didn't think it had a place in his talk because he pictured an audience who valued *product* over process, who wanted to hear about where he had arrived at rather than the journey there.

That way of thinking was also a big part of the success of his business and brand. When you reach out to a pro to achieve your weight loss goals, you're more interested in losing weight yourself than hearing about how the pro did.

But a speech about the work you do is different from the work you do.

It was the tweak he needed to get onto the TEDx stage.

That's why the journey is so crucial. The audience wants to arrive with you, wants to go with you, but they don't want directions. Avoid telling them what they think. Instead, tell them a story and let them finish the equation. As Andrew Stanton says in his TED talk, The Clues to a Great Story: "Give them 2 + 2 but not 4."

As a demonstration of how to establish credibility, consider the example of St. Paul from the Bible. If you're a little rusty on old St. Paul and his backstory, here's a refresher:

Great Speech!

Paul's section of the Bible is the one that comes right after the gospels—it's part of the New Testament, but Paul was born after Jesus and never met him. He's counted as an apostle, but he's not one of the original twelve. He didn't just miss the last supper. He hadn't even been born yet. Paul comes later and is responsible for figuring out the technical details about how it all works in early Christianity and for, well, spreading the gospel. This is what gets him apostle status and even into the Bible in the first place.

His origin story begins with him not being a Christian, but not even being named Paul. He starts out as a Roman named Saul.

This is where it gets interesting. Paul's story is a testament to the power of transformation and the impact of an origin story. It shows where you start and doesn't dictate where you end up. It also teaches us that the key to an effective story is not always the degree to which it features you as the agent of your transformation. Saul—later Paul—finds something he doesn't expect at a moment and in a way that he doesn't predict.

That's the template for the effective origin story. You weren't looking, but you found something anyway. Now, you have to tell everyone.

As we say to our clients, when you're putting your talk together, it's important to avoid what we call the Supervillain Syndrome. We've not yet worked with an actual supervillain, at least not so far as we know, but some clients inadvertently end up sounding a little like one, which, of course, is totally supervillain. From Lex Luther's perspective, he's one of the good guys.

There's no question our clients are amazing people like doctors and innovators who have improved the world, but

Build the Problem

sometimes their deep commitment to the work they're doing can shape the story they tell about in an unfortunate and unexpected way.

Remember, we're not talking about the work itself; we're talking about the most effective way of communicating why it's important. The one thing you can say for sure about supervillains is they are totally committed to their evil vision—no one sort of wants to kind of take over the world.

In the realm of storytelling, especially in the context of superhero and supervillain narratives, there's a distinct contrast in the way origin stories are crafted. Supervillains stand at the center of their own origin stories, seeking or creating the circumstances leading to their transformation. Their own involvement in their genesis is the hallmark of many supervillain backstories. They're the ones who delve into forbidden territory where an experiment goes awry and grants them supervillain powers. This self-initiated, self-made transformation is crucial to their character development, as it underscores their desire for control, and often, their out-of-control ambition.

We see this most often in the clients who have come out of the world of coaching. They tend to hold the moment when they turned their lives around as foundational to their sense of self. And it's that moment of taking the steering wheel of their own life that has a transformational impact. We're not skeptical of that process—both of us know the power of great coaching and that the sense of self-efficacy can truly change a life—but that doesn't mean it plays well onstage.

Heroes like Spider-Man almost always have an accidental or even reluctant entry into their superpowered life.

This makes sense as a story. No one wants a hero who has invested serious time and effort figuring out where and how to expose himself to radioactivity, carefully dangled an arachnid in exactly the right place at the right time, and then engineered getting bit by it.

For Spider-Man, it's *all* an accident. It's not just that the Spider-Man situation doesn't happen all that often, it's that it never happens. That's a key aspect of why we like Peter Parker, of why he's a sympathetic character: his journey isn't about seeking power but about dealing with its unexpected arrival, its moral dilemmas, its scheduling hassles, dating complications, and costume changes.

That's what makes us relate to him and like him, and it's no different with you and the great idea or insight that you want to share with the world. This accidental or even reluctant discovery of your idea makes for a compelling origin story because it avoids a chronological chain of events and just gets to the moment where you had agency. Where you had to make a choice. Where nothing would ever be the same. The turning point.

The reluctant hero is thrust into extraordinary circumstances and must-make choices. They don't want to save the world; they have to. Superheroes don't wake up super and brush their teeth in superhero ways. But the choices they make in moments that matter is what shapes them.

That's the kind of backstory you want, whether it's a keynote, or a TEDx talk, or any other kind of speech or presentation. The key to a compelling origin story lies in the unexpected. Find whatever it is that will make you the person you are going to turn out to be in a way that is unplanned, weird, or even unwelcome. Put the superhero—at least initially—in the position we're all in, more or less, which is trying to figure out what's next, where we're going, and how to get there.

You guessed it. It's time for assignment #5:

Answer these questions:

1. Why are you the person to help us solve this problem?
2. Why is it urgent that we solve this problem?
3. Why is now the time to solve this problem?

Still missing the blueprint? This is getting awkward. Download it here:

CHAPTER SIX

Solutions

When we were on that logo committee, we had no idea what the ingredients of a really great logo were—and that's what stood between us and our objective.

And so we brainstormed and brainstormed some more, and in the course of it, we not only became convinced that we had what it takes to create a great logo, we came up with a lot of ideas about what our logo *could* look like. That's the essence and point of brainstorming: to come up with a ton of ideas and capture them *all*, even if they're bad ones.

In the end, the final version of the logo didn't resemble any of the ideas that emerged from our brainstorming sessions, which is what usually happens.

Here's the thing: *most* ideas are bad ones. The vast majority of ideas are unoriginal. They're the first thing that pops into your head, which means that they're obvious—and obvious is the enemy of interesting. We all know that, yet when most of us sit down to write a speech, that's exactly where we start: with the obvious.

The way to start is *not* with an idea—it's with a *problem*. With something that you're trying to figure out, a mystery you're trying to solve. And that's true whether you're writing a speech or trying to come up with a logo or doing pretty much anything else in life.

Start with a problem, and then try to solve it. That's where your talk is headed, the destination. When it comes to speeches, the solution you're looking for is usually some version of this: what is the most important thing I want to say to this audience right now? What is the thing they need to hear? What is the thing I need them to understand? What gift do you want to give?

Once you've clearly articulated the problem, you can start to look for the answer. And the way to do that is *not* by brainstorming a bunch of ideas. It's by doing research. It's by looking at data. It's by talking to people who know more about this than you do. It's by reading everything you can get your hands on. In other words, it's by taking the time to actually figure out what the solution is, then using the stage to share your perspective.

If you're an expert in the field—and more often than not, it's expertise that has drawn you to the stage in the first place, because there's something that you're compelled to give to others—you are *ready* for this.

And in the work we do with clients, for us, this is actually the fun part. This is where the talk reveals itself. It's also where we often get to wow our clients, because we actually dig in with them.

As to what the solution part of your speech should look like, there's no one answer. The solutions are going to be as varied as the problems they seek to address. But there's one thing we've learned over the years, and that's when it comes to solutions, less is more. Way more.

Though we don't make a strict rule of it, our advice is to never conclude by offering any more than five solutions, though our recommendation is to limit it to three. If you have *one* entirely clear single solution, go with that. If it's two, give them both. But *not* more than *three*. Even if you have more and they're all great and crucial, even if you're absolutely certain that your audience needs to hear all fifteen of your carefully researched recommendations, see if they can't be more focused—if there can be *fewer* of them.

Why three? Because that's how many the audience is expecting without knowing they're expecting that number—which is to say because psychology (and fairy tales) tells us that three is the largest number of items that most people can hold in their memory. There are three little pigs and three bears for a reason.

This rule of three is everywhere once you start looking. It's in the structure of every joke (premise, setup, punchline), every story (beginning, middle, end), and every quest (three trials, three wishes, three chances).

It's Caesar's "Veni, vidi, vici." I's "life, liberty, and the pursuit of happiness.'" It's "blood, sweat, and tears." The ancient Greeks gave us the three Fates, Shakespeare gave us three witches in *Macbeth*, and Steve Jobs introduced the first iPhone by telling people it was three products in one: "An iPod, a phone, and an internet device."

Three is the number of completion, of wholeness, of something that feels both inevitable and surprising at the same time. When you give your audience three solutions, you're not just giving them a manageable number, you're giving them something that feels fundamentally right, even if they don't know why. You're tapping into a pattern that's as old as storytelling itself.

Solutions

But there's another reason to limit your solutions, and it's one we've seen play out more times on stage than we can count. When speakers offer too many solutions, they make their problem seem more insurmountable. It's the paradox of choice applied to problem-solving—give people too many options, and they're more likely to *not* choose any of them.

If you're giving a talk about climate change, for instance, and you list twenty things everyone needs to do right now to save the planet (which is actually a low number) you're not inspiring action—you're overwhelming your audience. They leave thinking, "The planet is toast anyway, so why am I taking out my recycling?" But if you focus on three clear solution steps, or fewer, it feels like the problems you can do something about.

Like everything else and despite being so fundamentally different from each other, the most effective and actionable solutions take a particular shape. There may be more than five—there are most definitely more than five—but these are the ones we see the most and which have the maximum impact

1. Mindset Solutions

These solutions focus on changing how people *think* about a problem. They're abstract but powerful because they lay the groundwork for all other changes. One of our clients, an executive business coach, offered what he called the "Acid Test" for goal setting. Instead of diving straight into action steps or habit formation techniques, his talk was about changing how people *think* about goal setting itself. As he told his audience: "The question isn't just whether you can achieve your goal, but whether you're willing to do what it takes to get there." What he offered was a mindset solution that fundamentally shifted how people approach achievement. That's a single, clear script the audience can follow toward success.

2. Individual Action Solutions

These are immediate, concrete *actions* that audience members can take as soon as they get to the end of your talk. The best ones are specific and achievable. Another of our clients, a conflict resolution specialist, offered what she called the "Curiosity First" approach. Instead of immediately defending your position in a workplace conflict, she gave her audience a distinctly different approach in the form of this single immediate action step: "The next time you're in a disagreement, before you respond, ask this question: 'Can you help me understand how you came to that conclusion?'" This isn't just general advice—it's a specific tactic that anyone can use in their next difficult interaction.

3. Systemic Change Solutions

These solutions target larger, institutional problems and often require collective action. We've already introduced you to the client of ours who's a surgeon—and surgeon coach—focused on medical errors, and what she offered at the end of her talk about how to prevent medical errors and save lives is a perfect demonstration of this. Her solution isn't just about individual doctor-patient interactions—it's about restructuring the medical consultation itself. She proposes implementing a mandatory, uninterrupted, two-minute patient-speaking time at the start of *every* medical consultation. This is a systemic change that can be implemented at the institutional level, yet it's specific enough that hospital administrators can envision exactly how to implement it. It's also something that *patients* can do—they can insist on their doctors taking the time (it's just two minutes!) to actually listen to them and not cut them off.

Pro tip: Systemic solutions work best in combination with action solutions, so that your entire audience can clearly see their role in it.

4. Behavioral Pattern Solutions

These focus on changing habitual behaviors over time. One of our clients works and consults in luxury hospitality—and much to our delight, her TEDx talk was selected as an "Editor's Pick." She was a former "young concierge of the year," which makes her an expert in human connection and relationship building. The throughline of her talk had to do with how we have to stop thinking that the way to make someone feel special requires us to invest in the most expensive or exclusive experience or gift, and start seeing how we *all* have the power to transform ordinary interactions into extraordinary moments. As she put it: "it's about paying attention. It's disrupting expectations that turns the ordinary into the extraordinary." Instead of just telling people to be more thoughtful, she provides a specific behavioral framework that transforms how people approach everyday interactions.

She also gives a three step process. First, identify daily routines and actively look for opportunities to disrupt them in meaningful ways. Second, develop what she calls "attention muscles" by actively noting and recording small details about people's preferences and patterns. Third, practice creative disruption by adding an element of imagination to ordinary interactions. What makes this such a powerful behavioral pattern solution is that it's both systematic and flexible. It gives people a clear process to follow while allowing for personal creativity in execution.

5. **Connection Solutions**

These solutions focus on transforming how we interact with others. One of our clients, who built a global tech company from scratch, offers what he calls the "People-First Triad." Instead of just advocating for better relationships, he provides a specific framework for transforming how we connect with others. This solution begins by showing how to make what he calls "the clear and deliberate decision" to prioritize connection by starting every interaction—whether it's a business meeting or casual conversation—with relationship-building rather than transaction.

If the solution you're offering has multiple steps, what's crucial is to present each of the steps in ways that complement each other. A common and effective shape we've used is to start with a mindset shift that changes how people *think*, followed by one immediate *action* everyone can take, and ending with one long-term solution that addresses the way the world works and brings about real *change*.

What makes this progression effective is that it builds—each step in the solution enables the next. The mindset shift helps people see that they don't need special resources or access to create memorable moments. This makes the immediate action feel *doable*—they can start right away with just one person. And once they experience success with that first interaction, they're more likely to adopt the systematic practice of paying attention and creating meaningful disruptions as an ongoing approach to all their relationships.

But having the right mix of solutions is only half the battle. The way you present them matters just as much. They need to be conveyed in ways that make them stick.

For example, another client of ours—a woman with a long and distinguished career in DEI consulting—had been selected by TEDx to give a talk about the superficiality of

Solutions

many diversity, equity, and inclusion (DEI) efforts. She could have just said outright that organizations need to take steps to make substantive change rather than approaching DEI as a box to be checked, but instead, she went back to her childhood and a doll she wanted to buy because she identified with its darker skin color. When she brought it to her mother, her mother refused, saying it was nothing but a "white doll dipped." That became a powerful metaphor to anchor the talk and illustrate the problem.

Just as her mother showed her that changing a doll's surface color doesn't make it authentically representative, she showed how superficial DEI initiatives that don't transform underlying structures are equally shallow. The metaphor works on multiple levels: it's personal (drawn from her childhood experience), visual (everyone can picture it), and emotionally resonant (it captures both the attempt at representation and its fundamental failure).

She reinforced this metaphor with another equally powerful one—comparing surface-level diversity efforts to "getting dressed for a workout, filling your water bottle, and grabbing your yoga mat, but never actually breaking a sweat." Both metaphors stick with you because they make the abstract concept of superficial change concrete through familiar, everyday images. They don't just tell us what's wrong—they *show* us, in ways we can feel and remember.

The power of these metaphors lies in their ability to capture complex ideas in simple, relatable terms. Just as a "white doll dipped" might look different on the surface while retaining all its original features underneath, many organizations' DEI efforts change surface appearances without transforming underlying structures. These images don't just explain the problem—they make it impossible to unsee.

But perhaps the most important thing we've learned about solutions is that they need to feel both aspirational *and* achievable. Your audience should leave feeling both inspired and equipped—like they've been handed both a vision and a toolkit. This is where many TED talks excel but where keynotes can struggle.

TEDx speakers are required to focus on one idea that can effect change in a short amount of time, which naturally leads to more focused solutions. Keynote speakers, often trying to cover more ground, can fall into the trap of offering too many solutions, none of which land with real impact.

To help our clients get past this, we have them list *all* their possible solutions—everything they think their audience needs to hear. Usually this list is long—*really* long. Then, we help them group these solutions into broader categories. Finally—and this is the hard part—we help them choose the three most important ones, the ones that will create the conditions for all the others to become possible.

The beauty of this approach is that it allows you to address solutions at multiple levels without overwhelming your audience. You're giving them something they can do today, something they can work on over time, and something they can strive for in the long term. Because make no mistake: being able to deliver a great speech is a game changer. It's one of the most effective ways to spread ideas, start movements, build your business, and change people's lives for the better.

Here's an exercise that will help you develop the solution section of your speech:

1. **Start with the problem statement you wrote earlier—you remember, the one phrased like this: "The problem is …"**

2. **Create three solutions that build on each other in a way that takes your audience on a journey from understanding to action.**

It's not uncommon for our clients to get stuck here, to hesitate for a moment as they think about which one, or more, of the many solutions that may have presented themselves to their imagination is the single solution.

Our advice is to not edit yourself, at least not right away. Instead, take the time to record *every* solution you can think of, to write down everything, from the obvious to the seemingly impossible. Include solutions you've tried, solutions you've seen others try, and solutions you wish existed.

As you're doing this, patterns are going to emerge that will allow you to group them into categories, or else the opposite will happen and you'll see that all the solutions cohere into a single solution. Whatever solution you hit on, make sure it's specific enough to be actionable but broad enough to be adaptable to different situations.

When you've done that, test your solutions by asking yourself these questions:

1. Can someone start implementing the solutions today?
2. Do they build on each other in a logical way?
3. Are they specific enough to be clear but flexible enough to be useful?
4. Do they address both individual and systemic aspects of your problem?
5. Do they feel both aspirational *and* achievable?

If you can answer yes to these questions, you have a solid solution section. If not, keep refining. Remember, your goal isn't to solve *every* aspect of the problem—it's to give your audience a clear path forward that they can actually envision themselves taking.

Assignment #6:

What are your top 3 solutions to this problem, and what's one thing anyone can do today?

You got that blueprint? Sheesh. You can lead a horse to water but you can't make him download the blueprint. Go on, download it here:

CHAPTER SEVEN

OMG Moment

Sixth is the OMG moment—and no, this one isn't about divine intervention, it's about the gift you're giving your audience. Think of it as the plot twist that makes everyone want to rewatch the movie. It's that gasp-inducing revelation that doesn't just end your speech but transforms how your audience sees everything that came before.

This is your Keyser Söze moment, your "Luke, I am your father," your "I see dead people." But unlike those twists at the end of movies, your OMG moment isn't about shock value—it's about *connection*. It's where you finally share the real reason you're on that stage, not the professional explanation in your speaker bio, but the personal truth that made this idea impossible to ignore. Most often, it's a story you've been holding back. Maybe it's something small that sparked a huge realization, or a gradual understanding that suddenly snapped into focus. Sometimes it's a prop that's been sitting there the whole time, or a detail in your story that seemed insignificant until this moment reveals its true importance.

The magic of the OMG moment is that it feels both surprising and inevitable. Your audience should experience that delicious double-take of "I didn't see that coming" and "Of course, it had to be this way." When you nail it, they won't just remember your speech—they'll be sharing it before it's even ended.

For us it's that logo. Remember that logo committee?

We never figured out the secret to making a great logo on that logo committee—although, years later, we have to say that we like the one that we came up with a lot. Okay, we love it. It did the job, and now we see it everywhere, and each time we see it, we get a sort of minor thrill knowing that we had a hand in its creation—but more importantly, what stays with us is what we figured out in that room about the nature of collaboration and the creative process.

After that first rush of confidence and enthusiasm we felt after first joining the committee, when it seemed, however briefly, that we were about to create the logo to end all logos, we got skeptical. Skeptical that we had anything to contribute but also skeptical that we needed experts in the room at all. Couldn't we do it in house? Why did we hire these people for something that we could bang out in a couple of hours?

But then, after it became clear to us that what we were banging out looked and felt banged out and was not the gleaming, perfect logo we were looking for, we reversed our position completely. If the logo folks did this for a living, we started to wonder, why didn't they just come up with one and hand it over? Did they actually need *us* in the room?

That wasn't about to happen, and after months of work, the whole thing seemed doomed to fail. We'd wasted hours of our time and a great deal of college resources all to come up empty-handed. The writing was on the wall.

There was one final meeting when it all came to a head. We were nearing the deadline, and we had to come up with something. The logo company presented their ideas, and we weren't impressed, and then they did the same with what we had come up with earlier in case we missed something, and the truth was those didn't work either. It was the most mediocre of stalemates.

There we were, looking at every iteration of the logo that we and the experts had produced over the course of six months. They had their favorite and made a strong pitch, but the committee wasn't convinced. Silence. The tension was palpable.

It felt awful, as if we had all reached the end of the line and were now facing the stark reality that we were going to have to report back to the college and admit that we had failed. We had to start again. We should fire the logo people and disband our committee and just tell the college that it could not be done.

In the movie version of the story—and we really hope there is *never* a movie version of this—there would be a cello playing followed by super sad close-ups of all of our faces. Some of us would shake our heads. There might be tears. The guy who had been on a hockey card would get up to get himself more coffee, but there would be no milk, and the absence of milk would convey how awful we all felt. We were about to break up.

Maybe there would be a montage that captured all that earlier optimism, the good times we had way back when we thought this was something that could be done. That we could do. A committee member actually stood up and started to leave the room, pushed his chair back in frustration, and shook his head. But then, just when it seemed as if there was nothing left to say, one of the members of the committee spoke up. "What if we took the front part of that logo and the end of that logo and brought them together."

The logo folk did it on the spot. Moved the elements around and all at once there was this feeling in the room.

That was it.

Even now, we're not sure how we got there, what we missed or what came together, or why it was so surprising and fresh and right, but that's what happened.

What we can see now very clearly in retrospect was that what made the process a success was that it combined their expertise with our experience of the institution, and the result was right and something none of us could have created on our own. It wasn't about expertise *versus* experience. It was about the power of collaboration.

That's the OMG moment of our logo story. It's the moment when we recognize our initial assumptions were wrong but in the best possible way. We needed the experts, but they also needed us. Our experience, our understanding of the college's culture and values, was just as crucial as their design skills and branding knowledge.

And before you ask—no, we're *not* going to show you the logo. Partly because lawyers exist, but *mostly* because it would be like showing you a photo of the Grand Canyon when what matters is the journey to get there. Besides, it's just a logo.

The real magic was in the *making* of it. Because that's what a great OMG moment does. It doesn't just repeat your main point; it elevates it. It takes your audience on a journey and reminds them of the journey by showing them how far they've come.

Unlike logos, which get redesigned every few years when someone decides they need a refresh, great speeches last forever. They become part of who we are. It's a moment of recognition, of seeing something familiar in a new light.

The most valuable thing to emerge from that day was a different, more nuanced, clear understanding of how collaboration worked and a new understanding of how to approach the creative process. We learned that listening is the most powerful tool in the collaborative process, that it's only by actually hearing what people are saying that new connections and possibilities emerge. While individual brilliance—the genius laboring in isolation, secreted away and insulated from others—has its place, there's also a power in what emerges when different people get put in the same room and are tasked with creating something.

Our fundamental mistake was thinking that there was an absolute or ideal or single way to create a logo, that there was a formula that we could feed our data into that would produce what we were looking for. If only we could get that, we would find it. But nothing of the sort exists, not when it comes to logo creation and not when it comes to writing a keynote or a TEDx talk. That's the nature of creating something. It doesn't exist until it exists. There's no ideal form of it.

But you're going to find it. You're going to make it.

What we missed—all of us, the logo experts *and* we, the subject matter experts who knew about the college—is we never saw the work of creating a logo as a creative process. It sounds ridiculous, but that's what happened. We were looking for the right answer to solve a problem.

We assumed that a logo was just another corporate task or that there was some predetermined right answer we were supposed to come up with. We had put in two plus two equals, and we thought we were looking for it to equal four, but when we came up with that, the expected, predictable answer, it felt entirely and completely wrong.

That is a mistake people make all the time. They come in having made up their mind already what the final version of their talk is going to look like, which doesn't leave any room for invention, for using the process to *discover* something. Your idea is the foundation of the talk you are going to give, but it's also going to be transformed by the process in ways that will surprise you.

If the outcome you reach at the end of the process doesn't intrigue *you*, it won't do that for anyone else. If the speech you create is precisely what you started with, you weren't following the blueprint. If we would have seen creating a logo as a creative process from the beginning, that our ideas are both informing and being shifted in the process of doing the work and doing it with each other, it wouldn't have been so painful. It wouldn't have taken us six months. And it wouldn't have had to force its way through at the very, very, very end, right when we were about to give up.

And that's our OMG moment.

Remember, it isn't about adding new information. It's about your audience seeing your message in a new light, making them *feel* something. In our story, the OMG moment wasn't when we finally saw the final logo. It was when we realized what it took to create that logo and what that process taught us about collaboration and the interplay between expertise and experience.

What revelation can you offer your audience? What new perspective can you give them on your topic? How can you make them see the familiar in a new way?

Because here's the truth: people will forget your statistics and your clever turns of phrase, but they'll never forget you helped them change their perspective. They'll never forget they experienced a transformation. And that's the power of a well-crafted OMG moment. It's your chance to give your audience a rush of realization. Go for something profound, give them hope, and give them something that changes *how* they think.

So, how do you create your own OMG moment? There's no one answer, but here's what you should consider:

1. **Share the exact moment when your mindset shifted.** Take your audience to that split second when everything changed—maybe it was a conversation that transformed how you saw goal-setting, or the instant you realized your assumptions were holding you back. Make it visceral. Make them feel the before and after. If your solution is about changing how people think about a problem, create a moment where you help the audience experience that change in real-time. Think about showing them the same scenario twice—once through the old mindset, once through the new.

2. **Make it personal.** Maybe it's your story, or maybe it's about someone or something else. Now is the time to tell it. When it comes to story, you need to think of it not as something that's nice to have but one of the most powerful methods of organizing experience and communicating content. There are any number of powerful ways to launch into a story, one of which is to simply announce it—"I'm going to tell you a story about how this matters." There's something that happens in the brain of audiences who know a story is on the way. Their attention shifts, and they start not just to listen but *really* listen. Another approach, often even more effective, is to drop your audience directly into the action: "The phone rang at 3 a.m." or "There I was, standing in front of two thousand people, and I had completely forgotten what I was supposed to say." You can also provide a quick framework—"Before this happened

to me, I was exactly where you are now"—that helps your audience understand why this story matters to them. Either way, your goal is the same: to make your audience lean in, to make them want to know what happens next.

3. **Consider using a prop or visual aid to make your point more tangible.** Think about Susan Cain's talk on the power of introverts (if you haven't seen it, you might be the only one), where she finally, when her talk is almost done, turns around and begins to unpack the mysterious bag that has been sitting beside her the whole time. She knows her audience has been sitting there, looking at it, that they watched her carry it out, that they've been wondering. Spoiler: she removes books from it, a concrete example of the power of introversion and of what introverts bring to the table. But it does more than just return us to the beginning—it transforms that moment of childhood shame into one of adult pride, connecting us to the hero of her talk, her grandfather, and all his favorite authors. In this way, the prop isn't just a visual aid—it's a bridge between past and present, between personal story and universal truth, showing us how what once seemed like a weakness has become a source of strength.

4. **Use something that returns**, like a recurring phrase or gesture, maybe even a prop, that evolves throughout your talk, demonstrating how small changes in behavior add up to significant transformation. Maybe start with an ordinary interaction and gradually layer in elements of attention and disruption. Stage a "pattern interrupt" that mirrors your solution. If you're

talking about disrupting routines to create extraordinary moments, create an unexpected moment in your own talk that demonstrates exactly how this feels.

5. **Use physical space and movement to demonstrate the type of connection that you've been advocating for in your talk.** Maybe it's a stronger or more profound connection, or maybe it's slower, more intentional—whatever it is embodies the shift you are trying to bring about. Take a common business scenario—maybe a standard meeting opening, maybe the kind of high stakes interaction that typically goes awry—and show how applying your connection framework completely changes the energy and outcome. Make it so tangible that people can't unsee the difference.

Assignment #7:

Tell a story that brings us back to the beginning of your speech with a new perspective. What did you leave out? Or what did you learn that you haven't revealed to us yet?

In marketing, they say you have to hear an offer at least 7 times before you buy it. Welp, this is free. Now get the blueprint!

CHAPTER EIGHT

Call to Action

Y ou're very nearly at the end of the book, but not quite, not entirely. This book is like a speech in that it doesn't just have an ending, but a *very* end, something after the end, a final call to action where you can imagine us lowering our voices, slowing down, getting extra real, and saying something like, "If there's one thing we could leave you with ..."

So here's our call to action.

We've gone through the blueprint, about how to start, how to establish the problem, the throughline, building the problem, how to craft solutions and OMG moments. If you've made it this far into the book, you're feeling more confident about your ability to put together a great speech that people will be completely captivated by. But before we wrap this thing up, we want to give you the permission to go forth and create something transformational.

Allow yourself to surprise yourself.

That is not to say that our advice is to ignore the rest of the book. The way to surprise yourself is to follow the structure we've outlined by understanding the building blocks—your

Call to Action

attention-getter, your problem statement, your throughline, building the problem, your solutions—but don't end there.

Be ready to recognize insight even when it doesn't fit your original plan. That's where innovation is born. And that's how you create something that doesn't just meet criteria but moves people. It can feel risky. It's not always easy to explain or justify an intuitive decision. But the payoff is worth the risk. You get a speech that feels authentic—that resonates deeply.

You're not going to craft a world-changing speech on your first try. It takes practice. It takes patience. And part of that work is collaboration. But most of all, remember that your speech isn't about you, it's about *them*. Your audience. This is incredibly freeing when you internalize it. It takes the pressure off.

You're not up there to show off how smart or clever or charismatic you are. You're there to serve your audience. When you approach speaking from this perspective, it changes everything. Suddenly, it's not about your limitations or insecurities. It's about the message you're trying to convey, the impact you're trying to make.

It's about something bigger than you.

At its core, your call to action needs to say very clearly how your audience can be part of solving the problem you started with. But there's a deeper way to think about this: What's the gift you want to leave your audience with? What's that one thing you want them to take away?

Here are three ways to deliver your call to action:

1. **Full Circle**

    Go back to that first question we asked you: What gift do you want to give your audience? Now answer these questions:

1. When I first started working on this problem/idea, what I wished I knew was ...
2. If I could go back and tell my earlier self one thing about this, it would be ...

Your call to action might be hiding in the gap between what you needed to know *then* and what you know now. That's the gift. That's what you're leaving with your audience, the one thing they'll take with them from your talk.

2. **The Legacy Question**

Another way to arrive at your call to action is to ask yourself what part of your talk you want to *stick* to those who hear it. Imagine it's ten years from now. Someone who watched your speech runs into you and remembers one thing from it—what would you want it to be?

1. The action they took?
2. The change this created in their life?
3. A single sentence that changed their perspective?

The most vivid and specific answer might be your "one thing"—the heart of your call to action.

3. **Permission**

Many really transformative and compelling calls to action involve giving the audience some form of *permission*—whether it's to change something in their life or the way they think, to get out of a relationship (or into one), to move from knowing that they need to do something and actually doing it. Find out if your talk is one of those by seeing if you can answer these questions:

1. What belief is holding them back?
2. What are they afraid of?

Whether you're giving a keynote or a TEDx talk, your call to action should feel like a gift, not a demand. It's the moment when you take everything you've shared—your expertise, your story, your solutions—and transform it into an invitation. It's where you say, "Here's what I want to leave you with …" and offer them the very thing you wished someone had given you when you first started this journey.

Assignment #8:

Go ahead and pick one of the three above that resonates with you, and then make it real—what's the first step your audience should take and can take today?

Here's another call to action … get the blueprint already!

CHAPTER NINE

The Secret Ingredient

Remember when we said there were seven ingredients to creating a great speech?

There are actually eight.

The eighth is delivery, and we know what you're thinking: "Wait, wasn't this book supposed to be *just* about structure?" It was, and it is. But think of it this way: structure is the foundation, writing is the house, and delivery is moving in and actually living there. We've given you the blueprint for a rock-solid foundation so that you can build the house. And we could spend another whole book on writing (and maybe we will), but delivery? That can't wait.

Whether your speech is next week or next year, whether your writing is polished or still rough around the edges, you need to know some fundamentals to stand up there and actually deliver the speech. Consider this chapter your emergency kit, your "go bag"—not everything you'll ever need, but it will get you started.

NOTE: We recommend getting private coaching for delivery work because of how nuanced each speaker's needs are, but before you do that, read this—especially if you've got a gig tomorrow.

1. Authenticity: Know Yourself and Don't Perform

Not even the most comprehensive list of ingredients results in an outstanding delivery. That's where the magic happens. That's where it clicks. That's where you go from giving a decent speech to delivering something that has your audience on the edge of their seats, nodding along, entirely with you the whole way, connecting with you and your idea in a way that they'll never forget.

Which means that one of the most crucial things is knowing yourself and delivering *as yourself*. Why? Lots of reasons. But one in particular, is that the average audience has become extremely adept at sniffing out things that are inauthentic, or derivative, pretending to be something that they are not.

It might have been all the reality television we consumed in the late 90s (and then every day since then) or the fact that social media dominates our attention, but people today are really sophisticated consumers of media—and that means we can spot *anything* that seems remotely "salesy."

Whatever it is, you've got to know your voice. You have to know who you are and be that person on stage, unapologetically. Without this understanding, your audience will check out. Guaranteed.

So, our advice is to lean into *you* and avoid the "schtick" that you may have seen another speaker use. Like a bunch of props, an interactive song, or lots of tech. It's not that these elements can never be effective, it's that most often the speaker is using them before the content of their speech works and that they're using them as a crutch.

If you use a tool like this eventually, and you probably don't need to, think of it as adding to an already effective speech, not as dependent on it, not as a substitution for creating, crafting, and delivering a great speech. Because the most likely consequence of using these tools ineffectively is that the audience ends up feeling that your speech is more about you than it is about them.

Another reason knowing yourself and your voice is important is that it will give you confidence on stage. Once you have a clear idea of who you are, when you're on stage in front of people, you can stand firm in your integrity and your expertise. You can be unequivocal. You can put your stake in the sand. Draw lines. You can be comfortable not pleasing everybody. Ultimately, it's the clarity of true confidence that draws attention and commands credibility and authority. A great speech doesn't ask for approval, it delivers it.

Here's one more way to think about this: The delivery of your speech is not a *performance*, it's a conversation. It's not a monologue, and it shouldn't feel like one. A mistake new speakers often make is getting on stage and putting on some artificial persona, mistaking the form as theatrical, or perhaps thinking that the harder they try, the more likely they are to captivate their audience.

Another cause of this is that they aren't confident in their content, so they want to perform it to compensate. What they really need to do is just be present and authentic. But, whatever you do, don't act. Acting is hard. That's why they give awards for it (and also because Hollywood loves to congratulate themselves).

Now, as we write this section about how your speech is a conversation and not a performance, there are public speaking coaches around the world psychically feeling the need to correct us and are preparing the draft of their negative review on Amazon—written in all caps.

First, let us say: *That's a bit performative.* But seriously, as a reminder for everyone, including our coaching friends, this book is about TEDx talks and keynote speeches that are rooted in your business or mission. They are tied to your industry or a transformative idea that will ultimately pull people in to learn more about you and your work.

So, while there are always exceptions, these kinds of talks really should be more of a conversation and delivered as such. Really. This doesn't mean there aren't venues where your speech or talk can be more performative in nature, like speaking competitions, personal storytelling stages, or that TikTok trend where … okay, we're not on TikTok, but you get the point.

All this being said, there absolutely are benefits to blocking (how you move or stand), or practicing your hand gestures, or otherwise elevating your persona on stage, but trying to learn and apply these elements on the fly for new speakers in a time crunch is going to do more harm than good. It will appear theatrical and rehearsed, and it will take the audience away from your message.

We've seen it over and over again. Do *not* spend more time on these elements than you do on developing your content and finding ease in your delivery. Talk the way *you* talk and move the way *you* move. If you have lots of energy, great, use that on stage. If you're more subdued and your humor is as dry as a popcorn fart in a desert … great! Use that, maybe. The point is that you are always you on stage. Your stage persona should be a slightly exaggerated version of yourself.

At the same time, being natural doesn't mean being unprepared. In fact, it requires *more* preparation, not less.

The key to being present and natural is to know your material cold, forward and backward, so that the words can flow naturally without you even having to think about it. There's a wise adage running through the speaking world that goes something like this:

If you're overly nervous, there are only two causes, you're either not prepared or you think it's about you. And it's probably both.

2. Vocal Variation: Pace, Pitch, and Pause

Authenticity is key, but it's not enough on its own. As you do more speaking and advance in your ability onstage, you'll also need to bring variation to your delivery. Change up your pacing, your pitch, the placing and length of your pauses, and more. Build to big, applause-worthy crescendos. Think of yourself like a great vocalist delivering a classic song—they know when to belt it out and when to pull back to a whisper. It's truly in vocal variation where audiences are moved to an emotional state and thereby moved to take action.

We've all had the experience of listening to a speaker who stays in the same tone and pace for the entire talk. If they're too upbeat the whole time, it's exhausting; if they're consistently slow and intentional, it's like a lullaby without the nap.

That's why vocal variety is essential—it keeps your audience engaged, helps them remember the best stuff, and prevents listener fatigue. Switch up your rhythm, pitch, and volume, and you're basically slapping them to attention every other sentence. Some people are naturally good at this. Most of us aren't. So here's a mini blueprint.

Start by being intentional. Go through your script, and highlight those big moments: the power lines, the key takeaways, the ideas that deserve a mic drop. You'll start to see where you can speed up before a powerful line, pause, speak, then pause again. Or where you can slow down and drop the pitch of your voice for a big reveal, then pick up the pace. Make these notes in your script. Come up with your own shorthand or color coding. These intentional little tweaks can turn "nice speech" into "you blew my mind!"

Variation in your volume, pitch, and tone are essential. You can completely shift your audience's focus and emotional state just by adjusting these. Variation in your volume is straightforward: speak louder to grab attention, go softer to build suspense. Pitch is the highs and lows in your voice. Variation in pitch keeps you from sounding like Siri. Try a higher pitch to convey excitement and a lower pitch when delivering something more sincere.

Tone is the emotion in your voice. It's what gives your words the right mood. A Dirty Hairy line like "Go ahead, make my day" has an unmistakable grit and seriousness to it. We can also see how the line has to be delivered in tandem with the right volume and pitch for full effect. Play around with these tools to keep the audience guessing and ultimately remembering your best lines.

Your pace is another secret weapon. Speed up when you're excited or when you're covering familiar ground. Slow down for a key point, or when you really want people to soak up what you're saying. And don't forget to pause—but not just any pause, a "pregnant pause." Hold it for a second longer than you think you should. It's the ultimate attention-getter. Pause at the start of your talk to build suspense. Pause after a major point to let it sink in. Pause before a punchline. Pause after you ask a question. Pause at the end. Basically, sprinkle … pauses … everywhere.

Another way to hold attention is to **vary your sentence length**. Mix short, punchy lines with longer ones. Again, go through your script and check your sentence length. If there's not enough variation, it's an easy fix. And while you're in there tweaking things, you might as well add a little repetition. In Steve Jobs' Stanford commencement speech, he said, "You can't connect the dots looking forward; you can only connect them looking backward. So you have to trust that the dots will somehow connect in your future."

By repeating the phrase "connect the dots" throughout his speech, it not only holds our attention but also makes it memorable and brings us back to his throughline. Or what about the "I have a dream" speech? Remember it? Of course, you do. Dr. King repeated "I have a dream" nine times in five minutes, each with a different pitch, volume, or pace. The simple tool of repetition helped it become one of the most recognizable speeches in human history. This is the power of vocal variety.

3. **But Seriously, What Do I Do With My Hands?**

First, don't worry about your hands too much. This is going to deviate again from what many speaking coaches and other books on speaking are going to tell you because for some reason, there is a love of hand gestures and the meaning that each conveys in the speaking world. Again, don't get me wrong, there's power in hand gestures—think about the message and emotion of a fist raised in the air on an Olympic podium versus a middle finger hanging out of a car window. There's a lot to be said here.

However, on stage, what's more important to think about is body language. Unless your hand movements are erratic and distracting, you probably don't need to practice choreographed times to gently clasp your hands or bring your fingers together to create a subtle diamond shape at waist level that both conveys power and openness.

You'll find that body language springs naturally from your message and from your own confidence and belief in what you're saying. If you've put thought and care into your content, then your body movements are going to naturally follow. This is what we want. This is a direct reflection of your own authenticity and will therefore be different from speaker to speaker.

You may find yourself nodding when you get a good response from the audience or shaking your head when citing something that's part of your problem statement. You might lean forward slightly to make a stronger point or smile when you've hit a punchline. When you're truly present, when you own your content, when you're fully confident, you will find your body reacting to what you're saying. When you achieve this state, your audience is captivated. They are on the edge of their seats, ready to be transformed and take the next step in your call to action.

Be mindful that your body language is read from the moment you step onto stage, or in some cases, from the moment your audience can see you. Perhaps seated at the panel table just off stage or in the lobby before the speech. Know that your audience will carry over any information they have before your first word.

So, be intentional with your body language, whether on stage or off, don't let your body language be up for interpretation. Use it to elevate your credibility, your content, and ultimately to lift your audience out of their seats.

Assignment #9:

Pick one delivery element that you feel you need to work on the most. What will you do to strengthen it?

Last chance to get the fill in the blank blueprint here!

Appendix
The Blueprint in Action

It's one thing to have a blueprint—to understand the ingredients that make up a great speech and how they work together in theory. But what does transformation actually look like? What happens when you take these elements we've been talking about and bring them to life?

What follows are examples of talks that started exactly where you are right now: with an idea, a blank page, and maybe a slight suspicion that what we've been saying about structure actually matters. These speakers completed the same assignments you've just worked through. They wrestled with their problem statements, crafted their throughlines, and discovered their OMG moments. Now their talks have over a million views or have been selected as the TED Talk of the Day or earned the coveted TEDx Editor's Pick, and—most importantly—inspired real change in the world.

We're not going to reproduce these talks in full. Instead, we'll give you a behind-the-scenes look at how they came together—the challenges, the breakthroughs, and our thinking as we helped bring each one to life. Because you're not just one speech away from sharing your idea—you're one great speech away from changing the world and transforming your business.

Great Speech #1

Does more freedom at work mean more fulfillment?
By Sarah Aviram
TED Talk of the Day - Elevated to TED platform

Watch the full speech here!

The speaker here is HR leader Sarah Aviram, a client of ours who was as thrilled as we were when her TEDx talk was elevated to the TED platform and selected as the TED Talk of the Day. When it was shared to TED's entire email list, it received 600,000 views in less than a week. What makes this talk so powerful is that she uses her personal experience to reveal the real challenges that hybrid work policies can't fix—and shows how to truly thrive at your job no matter where you are actually working.

Attention-Getter: "I was working on my laptop from a beautiful beach in Bal ... the swaying of the palm trees, my favorite tropical drink, and a warm breeze ... And yet, something felt off."

Problem Statement: "More freedom doesn't mean more fulfillment."

Appendix: The Blueprint in Action

Throughline: "If you hate your job in Houston, you will hate it in Hanoi. What really needs fixing is your motivation to do the work itself."

Building the problem: "After a few months though, when the honeymoon period was over, the novelty of working in all these places started to wear off. And I, and so many of my new friends, started to realize that traveling was just a band-aid solution for the real problems."

Solutions:

1. Minimize obstacles related to money, identity, and routines.
2. Optimize opportunities for growth and impact.
3. Prioritize joy in your career.

OMG Moment: "Esther Perel, world-renowned psychotherapist and relationship counselor says that 'in the West today, most of us are going to have two or three marriages or committed relationships. And some of us are going to do it with the same person.'"

Call to action: "Clarify and activate your motivations to do work you love ... you won't be running away anymore. You'll be running towards what you truly want."

Great Speech #2

Why Women Don't Sh** at Work
By Irina Soriano
TEDx Editor's Pick

Watch the full speech here!

This is one of our all time favorite TEDx talks, by our client Irina Soriano, which does something truly daring: it takes one of the most taboo topics—workplace bathroom habits—and uses it as a metaphor for larger issues facing professional women. It's amazing and was a TEDx Editor's Pick, but the truth is that we knew it was going to be wonderful from our very first conversation with Irina.

We don't remember exactly the first thing she said, but when we asked her the question we always ask at the start of the session about the "gift" she wanted to give her audience, her reply was, "I want to give them the gift of being able to take a shit at work." It took us a while to stop laughing, but when we did, we immediately saw the truth and power of her idea. What makes this talk particularly remarkable is how it uses humor to build a deeper argument.

Attention-Getter: "I would like to quickly prepare you that this is not your usual TED talk because this talk is full of sh*t. I will say the word sh*t roughly 70 times in 12 minutes, so buckle up!"

Problem Statement: "Women can go all day holding in our physical sh*t, and if that's not hard enough, additionally we are also holding onto all our mental sh*t—many of us have become numb to the physical and mental pain this can cause. That's a woman's life."

Throughline: "Society has long told women to keep their sh*t to themselves and handed us a rulebook that says, 'Hide your sh*t.' Sh*t is not limited to the physical kind, this includes our mental sh*t also."

Build the problem: "Forty-two percent of women said that there is NO chance they sh*t in the bathroom nearest to their office. They find another bathroom on a different floor with less traffic and less people they know."

Solutions: The "PEACE OF SH*T METHOD":

1. Discover your sh*t.
2. Unpack it.
3. Liberate your sh*t.

OMG Moment: "So, ladies, we're knee-deep in this together. We have been told to be quiet. We have been told to hide. We have been told to flush our sh*t and get on with our day as if it was a mere inconvenience. We need to stop holding on and liberate ourselves. It's time to change the expectations we are silently enduring and to own our experiences loudly."

Call to action: "It's in our collective vulnerability that women can find liberation. True freedom from any of these expectations comes when we unite and embark on our Mindshift journeys together ... because shared sh*t is lighter sh*t.

Great Speech #3

The Secret to Making Someone Feel Special
By Sarah Dandashy
TEDx Editor's Pick

Watch the full speech here!

Here's another example of the blueprint in action from one of the talks that we've been referencing throughout the book. Sarah Dandashy is a travel expert with over 18 years of experience in hospitality. She started off as a luxury hotel concierge, where she earned numerous accolades—including winning "young concierge of the year" at the Concierge Olympics (as she said to us, yes, it's a thing).

She's seen firsthand the power of small, thoughtful gestures, something easy to forget in a world that equates "special" with "expensive." The core of her idea was that the most meaningful experiences are often the ones that money can't buy—they're the smaller things that break us out of our routine, tiny, personally crafted moments of surprise that show the other person that you authentically see and appreciate them.

Attention-Getter: "I've spent a career on the hospitality frontlines ... 15 of them as a concierge. That's 5,475 days of standing in a hotel lobby. And yes, you see it all."

Problem Statement: "When we try to make others feel valued, or appreciated, or loved, too many of us fall into the trap of equating 'special' with 'expensive' or 'extravagant.' We exhaust ourselves—and empty our wallets—by following the traditional script—designer gifts, expensive dinners, exclusive experiences."

Throughline: "We all have the power to transform ordinary interactions into extraordinary moments. It's about paying attention. It's disrupting expectations that turns the ordinary into the unforgettable."

Build the problem: "We're in an era of unprecedented luxury ... There are personal butlers, pillow menus, ice hotels, underwater restaurants. And yet, despite all this extravagance, that's not what matters most."

Solutions:

1. Understand how to disrupt routine.
2. Pay attention to details.
3. Be creative and execute with care.

OMG Moment: A story of an executive and a therapy dog, again from a colleague of hers in hospitality. The colleague had seen that a long-term guest at her hotel, a high-level executive, had seemed stressed and disconnected. After hearing him telling one of his team how much he missed his dog back home, the colleague arranged for a local therapy dog to visit his room: "The transformation was immediate and profound," she tells us, "the moment he opened the door and saw the dog, he was like a different person."

Call to action: "Choose one person in your life … and do something unexpected to brighten their day. It doesn't need to be elaborate or expensive. It just has to be about them."

Great Speech #4

Why We Need Adult Sex Ed
Dr. Kelly Casperson
TEDx Editor's Pick

Watch the full speech here!

Here's a TEDx talk that takes on one of society's most persistent taboos—sex education—and transforms it from an awkward adolescent topic into an urgent adult necessity. Kelly had us hooked right from our first meeting with her exuberant, amazingly frank, high-energy mode of delivery. We do hope you take the time to watch all of these talks, but Kelly's is one that you have to see for a number of reasons, not least of which is her stage presence and her amazing fashion sense.

She comes out on the TEDx stage in an outfit that says, "buckle your seatbelts"—she wears a long, red, flowing dress, black Converse All-Star basketball shoes, and her blonde hair seems to be standing straight up, as if it's a little shocked at the subject matter. As you might imagine, we get a lot of questions about how one should or shouldn't dress for a TEDx talk, and the advice we always give is to "dress like yourself, but also appropriate to the subject matter." Kelly

Appendix: The Blueprint in Action

does precisely this. Her talk is a TEDx Editor's pick and deservedly so—she uses her medical authority, humor, and direct approach to make a traditionally uncomfortable subject both accessible and compelling.

Attention-Getter: "I'm here because of tears and a box of Kleenex. Three years ago, a woman was crying in my urology clinic. Sobbing—you know in that way that sounds hopeless … I can't help her. No idea what to do."

Problem Statement: "Without sex, none of us would exist, and yet here we are—expected to be experts with close to zero education."

Throughline: "Sex unites us all … and as long as it is taboo, we cannot be fully connected to ourselves and to each other … Adult sex education will unbreak the world."

Build the Problem: "Worldwide the rate of sexual dysfunction—I'm talking any gender—is as high as 40–50 percent, with the highest rate of distress in the midlife age range."

Solution:

1. Biology - understanding our bodies
2. Psychology - understanding our minds
3. Sociology - understanding our culture

OMG Moment: "Remember, pleasure and connection are the goals. Realize that when the mind and body come together in the present moment and thinking ceases, it can be as close to a transcendent spiritual experience as many people ever get."

Call to Action: "Nobody is so good at sex that they can't get better. If you're having bad sex, or no sex, it does not mean you're broken. Remember, good sex is a skill."

Appendix: The Blueprint in Action

Great Speech #5

The Power of Following the Leader
Ruben Gonzalez
1 Million + Views

Watch the full speech here!

Here's one of our most-celebrated and most-watched client talks—over a million views and counting—from four-time Olympian Ruben Gonzalez. The core of Ruben's idea was that the fastest way to achieve our goals is by letting go of our fear-based control and individualism, thereby becoming vulnerable, which allows us to follow our coach or leader's advice.

It's a TEDx talk that at first could be mistaken as a sports story but it transforms into a powerful lesson about humility, growth, and success with wide application and relevance. What makes this talk particularly effective is also what makes so many people watch it and share it—it uses Ruben's unlikely journey of becoming an Olympic luger as the way to challenge our assumptions about control and the meaning of success.

Attention-Getter: "Ever since I was a little kid, I wanted to be in the Olympics. But I'm not a great athlete, so I didn't think it was possible and didn't pursue it. Then, when I was 21 years old, I was watching the Olympics on TV. And I saw this little guy about five foot one."

Problem Statement: "Olympic coaches and business leaders agree that very few people want to follow the leader anymore. That's a problem because it keeps them from being their best."

Throughline: "Being in control feels safe. But being in control keeps you in your comfort zone. You can't improve if you're in a comfort zone. Letting go is scary, but letting go gets you out of your comfort zone so you can improve."

Build the problem: "I've always been very independent," he tells us, "that's a nice way of saying I don't like people telling me what to do. I like to be in control. Even so, before I went to Lake Placid, I promised myself that I would submit to my coaches' leadership. After all, who was I to question the Olympic coaches? But it was so hard for me to follow their advice, and I paid the price."

Solution: "What if the next time you're trying to achieve a big goal, you found somebody that had already done what you wanted to do? What if you let go and follow their advice right away?"

OMG Moment: "You don't lose yourself when you follow the leader, rather, you can become better than you ever were before."

Call to action: "You'd create a better life. You'd start a ripple effect of success. And together we'd make the world a better place."

Acknowledgments

To all those who helped bring this book together.

To Leanne Morgan

To Bon Allen

To Sarah Reeve

To Drew Slater

To Kary Oberbrunner and team

To Andrew Tarvin

To Dan Faill

To Paul Osincup

To Tia Graham

To Catherine Toomer

To Lisa David Olson

To Kathy Zhang

To Jillian Rigert

To Kelly Casperson

To the folks at Colorado College and Colorado Springs.

And especially to our clients: You have improved us more than we could ever improve your speeches. We've lost weight because of you, we've enhanced our dental care, made lifestyle changes to improve our wellness, changed our mindset, created better habits, become better parents, and made real the power of a single speech to change the world.

About the Authors

Cesar Cervantes is a speaker coach and speechwriter based in Houston, TX. He started his journey as a stand-up comedian, was featured on Comedy Central, and appeared in several Hollywood movies. He then taught comedy classes in the theatre department at Colorado College before becoming a professional speaker, teaching people how to develop deeper connections using humor. Cesar has served as a speaker coach at multiple TEDx locations across three continents. He now leads Top Talks and his speaker mentorship program. He's an avid tennis player and loves being a dad even more than he loves tacos.

Born and raised in Toronto, Canada, **Steven Hayward** is a Professor of English at Colorado College. In addition to publishing four award-winning books, including the Canadian national bestseller *Don't Be Afraid*, Steve is a seasoned keynote speaker, TEDx speaker, and directed the documentary feature The Block Plan, which won "Best Picture" at the 2022 Helsinki International Educational Film Festival.

WWW.GREATSPEECH.TV

THIS BOOK IS PROTECTED INTELLECTUAL PROPERTY

Instant IP™

The author of this book values Intellectual Property and has utilized Instant IP, a groundbreaking technology. Instant IP is the patented, blockchain-based solution for Intellectual Property protection.

Blockchain is a distributed public digital record that can not be edited. Instant IP timestamps the author's ideas, creating a smart contract, thus an immutable digital asset that proves ownership and establishes a first to use / first to file event.

Protected by Instant IP ™

LEARN MORE AT INSTANTIP.TODAY

Made in United States
Troutdale, OR
04/20/2025